Unit Assessments

mheducation.com/prek-12

Copyright © McGraw-Hill Education

All rights reserved. The contents, or parts thereof, may be reproduced in print form for non-profit educational use with *Wonders*, provided such reproductions bear copyright notice, but may not be reproduced in any form for any other purpose without the prior written consent of McGraw-Hill Education, including, but not limited to, network storage or transmission, or broadcast for distance learning.

Send all inquiries to:
McGraw-Hill Education
Two Penn Plaza
New York, New York 10121

ISBN: 978-0-07-901760-4
MHID: 0-07-901760-6

Printed in the United States of America.

1 2 3 4 5 6 QVS 23 22 21 20 19   A

Table of Contents

Teacher Introduction iv

Unit 1
Assessment 1
Performance Task 19

Unit 2
Assessment 27
Performance Task 43

Unit 3
Assessment 51
Performance Task 68

Unit 4
Assessment 77
Performance Task 95

Unit 5
Assessment 103
Performance Task 120

Unit 6
Assessment 131
Performance Task 147

Answer Keys and Rationales
Unit 1 159
Unit 2 168
Unit 3 176
Unit 4 184
Unit 5 191
Unit 6 200

Teacher Introduction

Unit Assessments

The *Unit Assessments* component is an integral part of the complete assessment program aligned with *Wonders* and state standards.

Purpose

This component reports on the outcome of student learning. As students complete each unit of the reading program, they will be assessed on their understanding of key instructional content and their ability to write to source texts/stimuli. The results serve as a summative assessment by providing a status of current achievement in relation to student progress through the curriculum. The results of the assessments can be used to inform subsequent instruction, aid in making leveling and grouping decisions, and point toward areas in need of reteaching or remediation.

Focus

Unit Assessments focuses on key areas of English Language Arts—comprehension of literature and informational text, vocabulary acquisition and use, command of the conventions of the English language, and genre writing in response to sources.

Each unit assessment also provides students familiarity with the item types, the test approaches, and the increased rigor associated with the advances in state-mandated high-stakes assessments.

Test Administration

Each unit assessment should be administered once the instruction for the specific unit is completed. Make copies of the unit assessment for the class. You will need copies of the answer key pages that feature the scoring charts for each student taking the assessment, which provide a place to list student scores. The data from each unit assessment charts student progress and underscores strengths and weaknesses.

This component is the pencil-and-paper version of the assessment. You can administer the online version of the test, which allows for technology-enhanced item functionality.

NOTE: Due to time constraints, you may wish to administer the unit assessment over multiple days. For example, students can complete the 20-item test on the first day and complete the performance task on another. For planning purposes, the recommended time for each performance task is 90–100 minutes over two back-to-back sessions. During the first session, provide students 30–40 minutes to read the stimulus materials and answer the research questions. During the second session, provide students 60–70 minutes for planning, writing, and editing their responses. If desired, provide students a short break between sessions. If you decide to break-up administration by assessment sections, please remember to withhold those sections of the test students are not completing to ensure test validity.

After each student has a copy of the assessment, provide a version of the following directions:

Teacher Introduction

Say: *Write your name on the question pages for this assessment.* (When students are finished, continue with the directions.) *You will read three texts and answer questions about them. In the next part of the test, you will read a student draft that you will revise or edit for the correct grammar, mechanics, and usage. In the final part of the test, you will read sources, answer questions about them, and write a response based on the assignment you will find, which will ask you to use those sources in your writing.*

Read each part of the test carefully. For multiple-choice questions, circle the letter next to the correct answer or answers. For other types of questions, look carefully at the directions. You may be asked to match items, circle or underline choices, or complete a chart. For the constructed-response question, write your response on the lines provided. For the performance task, write your response to the assignment on separate sheets of paper. When you have completed the assessment, put your pencil down and turn the pages over. You may begin now.

Answer procedural questions during the assessment, but do not provide any assistance on the items or selections. Have extra paper on hand for students to use for their performance task responses. After the class has completed the assessment, ask students to verify that their names are written on the necessary pages.

Assessment Items

Unit assessments feature the following item types—selected response (SR), multiple selected response (MSR), evidence-based selected response (EBSR), constructed response (CR), and technology-enhanced items (TE). (Please note that the print versions of TE items are available in this component; the full functionality of the items is available only through the online assessment.) This variety of item types provides multiple methods of assessing student understanding, allows for deeper investigation into skills and strategies, and provides students an opportunity to become familiar with the kinds of questions they will encounter in state-mandated summative assessments.

Performance Tasks

Each unit features a performance task (PT) assessment in a previously taught genre. Students will complete two examples of each task type by the end of the year.

- Narrative
  - Students craft a narrative using information from the sources.

- Informational
  - Students generate a thesis based on the sources and use information from the sources to explain this thesis.

- Opinion
  - Students analyze the ideas in sources and make a claim that they support using the sources.

Each PT assesses standards that address comprehension, research skills, genre writing, and the use of standard English language conventions (ELC). The stimulus texts and research questions in each task build toward the goal of the final writing topic.

Teacher Introduction

Overview

- Students will read three texts in each assessment and respond to items focusing on comprehension skills, literary elements, text features, and vocabulary strategies. These items assess the ability to access meaning from the text and demonstrate understanding of unknown and multiple-meaning words and phrases.
- Students will then read a student draft that requires corrections or clarifications to its use of the conventions of standard English language or complete a cloze passage that requires correct usage identification.
- Students are then presented with a performance task assessment.

Each test item in *Unit Assessments* (as well as in progress monitoring and benchmark assessments) has a Depth of Knowledge (DOK) level assigned to it.

Vocabulary items

DOK 1: Use word parts (affixes, roots) to determine the meaning of an unknown word.

DOK 2: Use context or print/digital resources to determine the meaning of an unknown or multiple-meaning word; use context to understand figurative language.

Comprehension items

DOK 1: Identify/locate information in the text.

DOK 2: Analyze text structures/literary elements.

DOK 3: Make inferences using text evidence and analyze author's craft.

DOK 4: Respond using multiple texts.

Revising and Editing items

DOK 1: Edit to fix errors

DOK 2: Revise for clarity and coherence.

Each unit assessment features three "cold reads" on which the comprehension and vocabulary assessment items are based. These selections reflect the unit theme and genre-studies to support the focus of the classroom instruction. Texts fall within the Lexile band 740L–940L. Complexity on this quantitative measure grows throughout the units, unless a qualitative measure supports text placement outside a lockstep Lexile continuum.

Comprehension

Comprehension items assess student understanding of the text through the use of the comprehension skills, literary elements, and text features taught throughout the unit.

Teacher Introduction

Vocabulary

Vocabulary items ask students to demonstrate their ability to uncover the meanings of unknown and multiple-meaning words and phrases using vocabulary strategies.

English Language Conventions

Five items in each unit ask students to demonstrate their command of the conventions of standard English.

Performance Task

Students complete one performance task per unit, which includes research questions and a final written response in the specified task genre.

Scoring

Each unit assessment totals 35 points. Comprehension and vocabulary items are worth two points each. Constructed-response and multi-part items should be answered correctly in full, though you may choose to provide partial credit. Revising and editing items are worth one point each. Use the scoring chart at the bottom of the answer key to record each student's score. Note that the performance task is scored separately, as described below.

For the constructed-response items, assign a score using the correct response parameters provided in the answer key along with the scoring rubrics shown below. Responses that show a complete lack of understanding or are left blank should be given a *0*.

Short Response Score 2: The response is well-crafted and concise and shows a thorough understanding of the underlying skill. Appropriate text evidence is used to answer the question.

Short Response Score 1: The response shows partial understanding of the underlying skill. Text evidence is featured, though examples are too general.

Each unit performance task is a separate 15-point assessment. The three research items are worth a total of five points, broken down as indicated in the scoring charts. Score the written response holistically on a 10-point scale using the rubrics on the following pages:

- 4 points for purpose/organization [P/O]
- 4 points for evidence/elaboration [E/E] or development/elaboration [D/E]
- 2 points for English language conventions [C]
- **Unscorable** or **0-point** responses are unrelated to the topic, illegible, contain little or no writing, or show little to no command of the conventions of standard English.

Use the top-score anchor paper response provided in the answer key for each test for additional scoring guidance.

Teacher Introduction

NARRATIVE PERFORMANCE TASK SCORING RUBRIC

Score	Purpose/Organization	Development/Elaboration	Conventions
4	• **fully sustained** organization; **clear** focus • effective, unified plot • effective development of setting, characters, point of view • transitions clarify relationships between and among ideas • logical sequence of events • effective opening and closing	• **effective** elaboration with details, dialogue, description • clear expression of experiences and events • effective use of relevant source material • effective use of various narrative techniques • effective use of sensory, concrete, and figurative language	
3	• **adequately sustained** organization; **generally maintained** focus • evident plot with loose connections • adequate development of setting, characters, point of view • adequate use of transitional strategies • adequate sequence of events • adequate opening and closing	• **adequate** elaboration with details, dialogue, description • adequate expression of experiences and events • adequate use of source material • adequate use of various narrative techniques • adequate use of sensory, concrete, and figurative language	
2	• **somewhat sustained** organization; **uneven** focus • inconsistent plot with evident flaws • uneven development of setting, characters, point of view • uneven use of transitional strategies, with little variety • weak or uneven sequence of events • weak opening and closing	• **uneven** elaboration with **partial** details, dialogue, description • uneven expression of experiences and events • vague, abrupt, or imprecise use of source material • uneven, inconsistent use of narrative technique • partial or weak use of sensory, concrete, and figurative language	• **adequate** command of spelling, capitalization, punctuation, grammar, and usage • few errors
1	• **basic** organization; **little or no** focus • little or no discernible plot; may just be a series of events • brief or no development of setting, characters, point of view • few or no transitional strategies • little or no organization of event sequence; extraneous ideas • no opening and/or closing	• **minimal** elaboration with **few or no** details, dialogue, description • confusing expression of experiences and events • little or no use of source material • minimal or incorrect use of narrative techniques • little or no use of sensory, concrete, and figurative language	• **partial** command of spelling, capitalization, punctuation, grammar, and usage • some patterns of errors

Teacher Introduction

INFORMATIONAL PERFORMANCE TASK SCORING RUBRIC

Score	Purpose/Organization	Evidence/Elaboration	Conventions
4	• **effective** organizational structure • clear statement of main idea based on purpose, audience, task • consistent use of various transitions • logical progression of ideas	• **convincing** support for main idea; **effective** use of sources • integrates comprehensive evidence from sources • relevant references • effective use of elaboration • audience-appropriate domain-specific vocabulary	
3	• **evident** organizational structure • adequate statement of main idea based on purpose, audience, task • adequate, somewhat varied use of transitions • adequate progression of ideas	• **adequate** support for main idea; **adequate** use of sources • some integration of evidence from sources • references may be general • adequate use of some elaboration • generally audience-appropriate domain-specific vocabulary	
2	• **inconsistent** organizational structure • unclear or somewhat unfocused main idea • inconsistent use of transitions with little variety • formulaic or uneven progression of ideas	• **uneven** support for main idea; **limited** use of sources • weakly integrated, vague, or imprecise evidence from sources • references are vague or absent • weak or uneven elaboration • uneven domain-specific vocabulary	• **adequate** command of spelling, capitalization, punctuation, grammar, and usage • few errors
1	• **little or no** organizational structure • few or no transitions • frequent extraneous ideas; may be formulaic • may lack introduction and/or conclusion • confusing or ambiguous focus; may be very brief	• **minimal** support for main idea; **little or no** use of sources • minimal, absent, incorrect, or irrelevant evidence from sources • references are absent or incorrect • minimal, if any, elaboration • limited or ineffective domain-specific vocabulary	• **partial** command of spelling, capitalization, punctuation, grammar, and usage • some patterns of errors

Teacher Introduction

OPINION PERFORMANCE TASK SCORING RUBRIC

Score	Purpose/Organization	Evidence/Elaboration	Conventions
4	• **effective** organizational structure; **sustained** focus • consistent use of various transitions • logical progression of ideas • effective introduction and conclusion • clearly communicated opinion for purpose, audience, task	• **convincing** support/evidence for main idea; **effective** use of sources; **precise** language • comprehensive evidence from sources is integrated • relevant, specific references • effective elaborative techniques • appropriate domain-specific vocabulary for audience, purpose	
3	• **evident** organizational structure; **adequate** focus • adequate use of transitions • adequate progression of ideas • adequate introduction and conclusion • clear opinion, mostly maintained, though loosely • adequate opinion for purpose, audience, task	• **adequate** support/evidence for main idea; **adequate** use of sources; **general** language • some evidence from sources is integrated • general, imprecise references • adequate elaboration • generally appropriate domain-specific vocabulary for audience, purpose	
2	• **inconsistent** organizational structure; **somewhat sustained** focus • inconsistent use of transitions • uneven progression of ideas • introduction or conclusion, if present, may be weak • somewhat unclear or unfocused opinion	• **uneven** support for main idea; **partial** use of sources; **simple** language • evidence from sources is weakly integrated, vague, or imprecise • vague, unclear references • weak or uneven elaboration • uneven or somewhat ineffective use of domain-specific vocabulary for audience, purpose	• **adequate** command of spelling, capitalization, punctuation, grammar, and usage • few errors
1	• **little or no** organizational structure or focus • few or no transitions • frequent extraneous ideas are evident; may be formulaic • introduction and/or conclusion may be missing • confusing opinion	• **minimal** support for main idea; **little or no** use of sources; **vague** language • source material evidence is minimal, incorrect, or irrelevant • references absent or incorrect • minimal, if any, elaboration • limited or ineffective use of domain-specific vocabulary for audience, purpose	• **partial** command of spelling, capitalization, punctuation, grammar, and usage • some patterns of errors

Teacher Introduction

Evaluating Scores

The answer keys have been constructed to provide the information you need to aid your understanding of student performance, as well as individualized instructional and intervention needs.

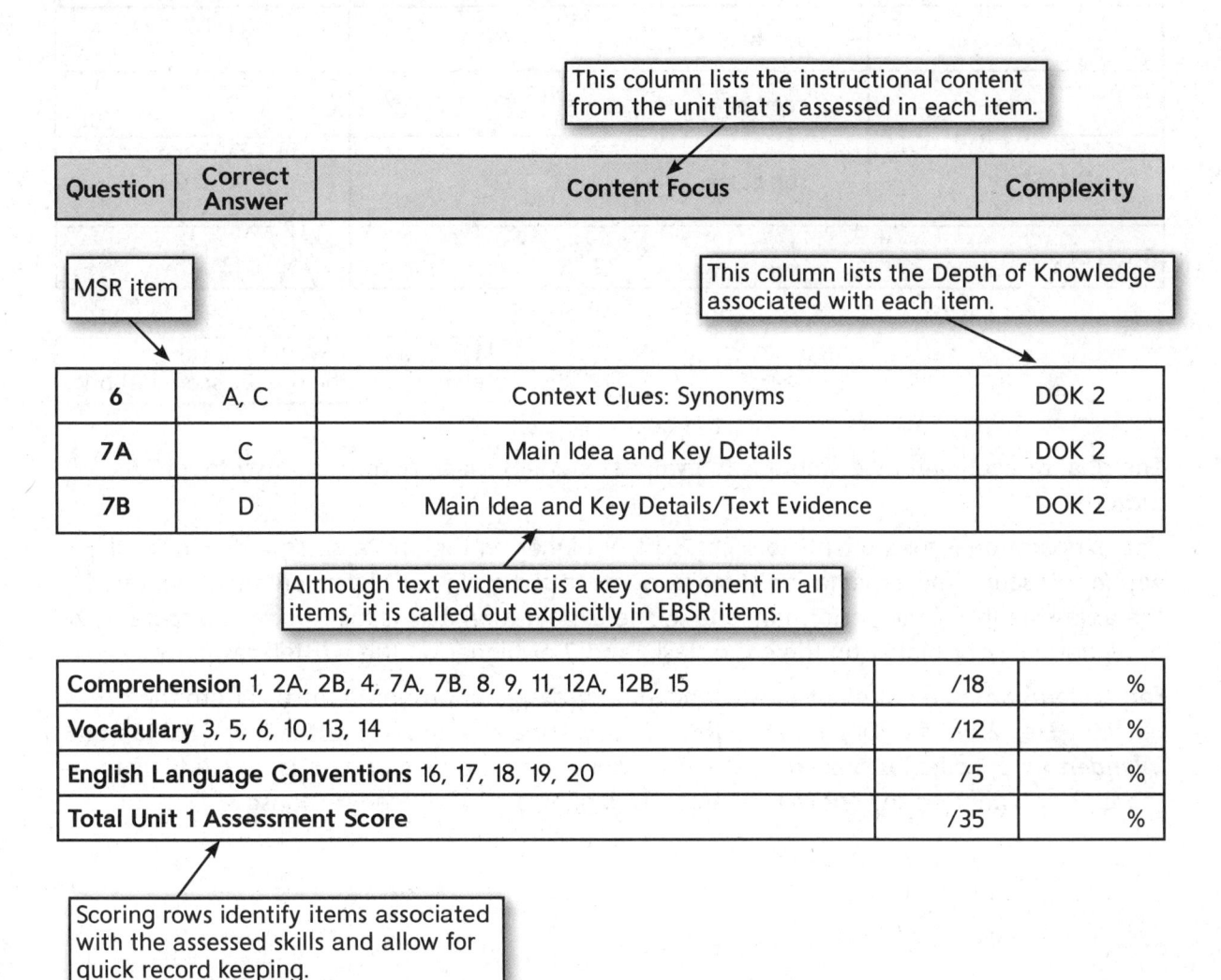

This column lists the instructional content from the unit that is assessed in each item.

Question	Correct Answer	Content Focus	Complexity

MSR item

This column lists the Depth of Knowledge associated with each item.

Question	Correct Answer	Content Focus	Complexity
6	A, C	Context Clues: Synonyms	DOK 2
7A	C	Main Idea and Key Details	DOK 2
7B	D	Main Idea and Key Details/Text Evidence	DOK 2

Although text evidence is a key component in all items, it is called out explicitly in EBSR items.

Comprehension 1, 2A, 2B, 4, 7A, 7B, 8, 9, 11, 12A, 12B, 15	/18	%
Vocabulary 3, 5, 6, 10, 13, 14	/12	%
English Language Conventions 16, 17, 18, 19, 20	/5	%
Total Unit 1 Assessment Score	/35	%

Scoring rows identify items associated with the assessed skills and allow for quick record keeping.

Unit Assessments — Grade 4 • Teacher Introduction — xi

Teacher Introduction

Narrative Performance Task			
Question	Answer	Complexity	Score
1	see below	DOK 2	/1
2	see below	DOK 3	/2
3	see below	DOK 3	/2
Story	see below	DOK 4	/4 [P/O] /4 [D/E] /2 [C]
Total Score			/15

This scoring row identifies the elements of the holistic scoring rubric.

The goal of each unit assessment is to evaluate student mastery of previously taught material.

The expectation is for students to score 80% or higher on the unit assessment as a whole; within this score, the expectation is for students to score 75% or higher on each section of the assessment. For the performance task, the expectation also is for students to score 80% or higher, or 12 or higher on the entire task, and 8 or higher on the written response.

For students who do not meet these benchmarks, assign appropriate lessons from the relevant **Tier 2 online PDFs**. Refer to the unit assessment pages in the Teacher's Edition of *Wonders* for specific lessons. For the performance task, the expectation is for students to score 12 or higher on the entire task and 8 or higher on the written response.

Read the passage. Then answer the questions.

Communicating Coast to Coast

In 1850, the United States Congress passed a bill making California the thirty-first state. It took nine weeks for the news to reach California. Today, news like that would zoom across the country in an instant.

Traveling to the West

Gold was discovered in California in 1848. This caused many Americans to head to the West Coast in search of fortunes. It was known as the "gold rush," but no one got there quickly. The cheapest way to travel west was by covered wagon. It was also the slowest. A wagon trip from St. Louis, Missouri, took about six months.

Some people traveled by sea. Ships sailed around South America. The trip from New York City to San Francisco was more than 16,000 miles. One ship made the trip in 89 days in 1851, but people wanted faster ways to travel.

More important, they wanted faster ways to send information.

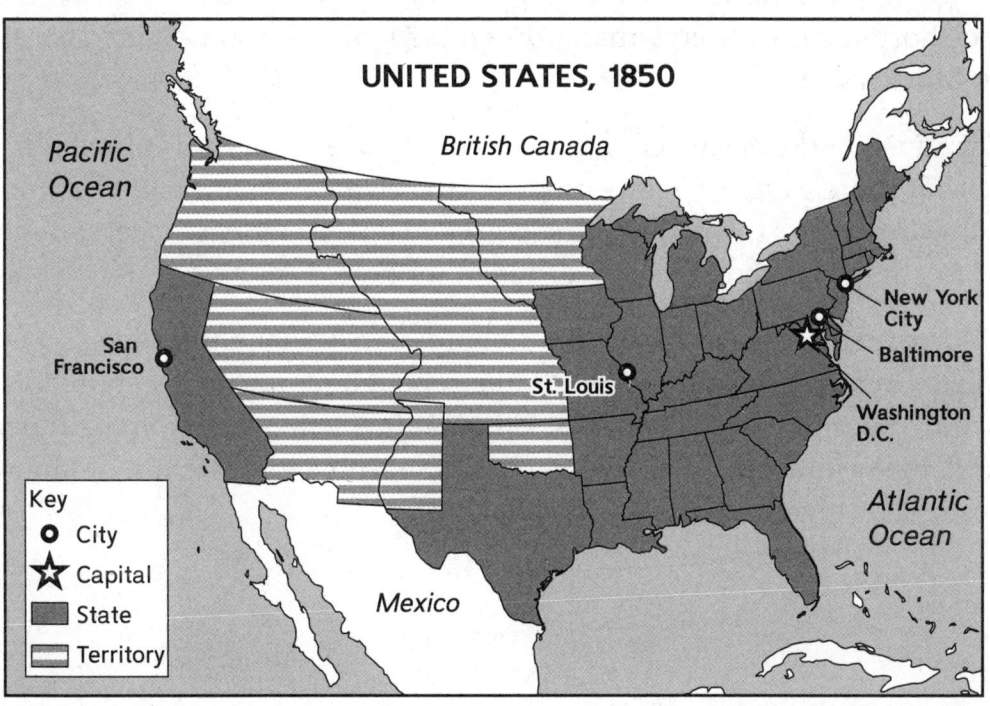

GO ON →

UNIT 1

Carrying the Mail

In 1858, stagecoaches began carrying mail. Letters traveled from St. Louis to San Francisco in just twenty-five days. Soon the mail traveled even faster when carried on horseback. The Pony Express was a series of stations across the West. Riders on horseback carried a pouch of mail from one station to the next. The first rider handed the mail pouch to the next rider, who rode off at great speed. At the next station, the pouch was handed off again. The pouch was handed off at several points until it reached the final station.

The Pony Express helped information travel more quickly. However, a revolutionary change in the way messages traveled was already taking place. A man named Samuel Morse was leading the way.

Connecting East and West

Morse overheard people discussing whether it would be possible to send messages along a wire. The idea excited him. He knew electricity traveled along a wire in an instant. Imagine sending messages that way!

His inventive mind got right to work. Morse soon had a working model of a telegraph. This machine started and stopped the flow of electricity. This created long and short bursts of energy that represented letters and numbers. This alphabet is called Morse code.

Morse dreamed of the day when messages could travel thousands of miles in minutes. But there were still many problems to solve. It would not be easy to string telegraph wires across the nation. Morse needed a lot of money to get it done. He decided to ask the United States government for help.

When Morse first presented his idea to Congress, they thought his idea seemed impossible. Eventually, Congress gave Morse enough money to get started. He demonstrated how the telegraph worked by sending a message from Baltimore, Maryland, to Washington, D.C. It worked! Those who had made fun of him were convinced. They regretted having ridiculed him.

GO ON →

Connecting the nation from coast to coast by telegraph was a big job. Finally, in 1861, wires from the East joined wires from the West, and the transcontinental telegraph was complete! As soon as the telegraph reached completely across the continent, news traveled at lightning speed. This led to the end of the Pony Express because even the fastest horses were no match for the telegraph.

Into the Future

Most telegraph messages were short. Because telegraph offices were not located in every town, many people still sent family news through the mail. Still, the telegraph paved the way for today's high-speed world of telephones, cell phones, text messages, television, radio, and the Internet.

Student Name _____

1. The following question has two parts. First, answer part A. Then, answer part B.

   Part A: What is the main idea of the passage?

   A Many people participated in the gold rush.

   B Methods of communication improved after 1850.

   C It took a long time for people to travel around in 1850.

   D The telegraph replaced other means of communication.

   Part B: Which sentence from the passage **best** supports your answer in part A?

   A "This caused many Americans to head to the West Coast in search of fortunes."

   B "The trip from New York City to San Francisco was more than 16,000 miles."

   C "Finally, in 1861, wires from the East joined wires from the West, and the transcontinental telegraph was complete!"

   D "Still, the telegraph paved the way for today's high-speed world of telephones, cell phones, text messages, television, radio, and the Internet."

2. The following question has two parts. First, answer part A. Then, answer part B.

   Part A: What is the **best** reason why people would prefer using the telegraph over the Pony Express to communicate?

   A because pony rentals were expensive

   B because no one believed Morse could invent his machine

   C because telegraph offices were not located in every town

   D because it was a faster method of communication

GO ON →

Student Name _____

Part B: Which sentence from the passage **best** supports your answer in part A?

A "The cheapest way to travel west was by covered wagon."

B "More important, they wanted faster ways to send information."

C "When Morse first presented his idea to Congress, they thought his idea seemed impossible."

(D) "This led to the end of the Pony Express because even the fastest horses were no match for the telegraph."

3   Read the sentence from the passage.

In 1850, the United States Congress passed a bill making California the thirty-first state.

What does the word passed mean in the sentence?

(A) to allow to go through

B   to complete successfully

C   to happen

D   to not notice

4   The following question has two parts. First, answer part A. Then, answer part B.

Part A: Read the sentence from the passage.

This caused many Americans to head to the West Coast in search of fortunes.

What does the word head mean in the sentence?

A   a body part attached to the neck

B   the top of an object

(C) to go toward

D   a person in charge of something

GO ON →

Student Name _____

Part B: Which sentence from the passage **best** supports your answer in part A?

A "Gold was discovered in California in 1848."

B "It was known as the 'gold rush,' but no one got there quickly."

C "It was also the slowest."

D "More important, they wanted faster ways to send information."

5   Complete the chart to match the causes from the passage with their effects. Mark **one** box next to **each** cause.

	Effect: The working model of a telegraph was invented.	Effect: News was able to travel at lightning speed.	Effect: The Pony Express was created to send letters in 25 days.
Cause: People wanted faster ways to send information out West.	☐	☐	☒
Cause: Morse overheard people discussing whether it was possible to send messages along a wire.	☒	☐	☐
Cause: Telegraph wires connected the East Coast to the West Coast.	☐	☒	☐

GO ON →

Read the passage. Then answer the questions.

A Mountain Dream

For years, Lisa Ricci had worked in her family's New York City bakery. She had enjoyed learning about the baking business. She loved seeing how many customers came back week after week for more, and she often handed children free sugar cookies just to see the smiles on their faces.

But Lisa was ready for an adventure. She liked New York, but the tall buildings couldn't hide the fact that the city was flat. Lisa yearned for a future that wasn't laid out and stretched thin before her like rolled dough. Lisa dreamed of the Rocky Mountains. Her friend Cindy Hooper owned a bed and breakfast in Colorado. Cindy invited Lisa to come work with her. Lisa imagined exploring the snow-capped peaks of the Rockies. She wanted to picnic in valleys filled with golden Aspen trees, dip her toes in cool, clear rivers, and watch elk feed at dusk.

In late summer, Lisa moved to Colorado, and she and Cindy agreed on a work schedule. Lisa would work Wednesday through Sunday, which sounded perfect. On her days off, she would go hiking in the Rockies. Lisa was so excited! She could hardly believe her luck.

One week into her new job, the luck that brought her to Colorado seemed to change. While changing a light bulb, Cindy fell from a stepladder and broke her leg. Cindy's leg would be in a cast for three months. Lisa wouldn't think of leaving her dear friend high and dry, so she toiled around the clock.

Lisa never complained. Months went by, and Lisa hadn't gone to the mountains once. There was a chill in the air, and soon winter would arrive. Lisa wouldn't have another chance to hike until spring. She was so close to the Rocky Mountains, and yet she couldn't seem to reach them.

Three months passed. Cindy's leg healed, and her cast came off. Finally, Lisa felt she could go off and explore. She joined Happy Trails Hiking Club. The club had organized a day hike that Monday in Estes Park. All Lisa had to do was walk three blocks to the corner and board a bus by 10 a.m. That would work just fine. Lisa told Cindy she would serve breakfast on Monday, even though it was her day off. Breakfast always ended at 9:30, so she would still have time to catch the bus.

GO ON →

UNIT 1

Lisa cleaned up the last of the breakfast dishes and wiped down the tables. At 9:45, she buttoned up her coat, filled her water bottle, and laced up her hiking boots.

Just as she was about to leave, two guests came downstairs. "Are we too late for breakfast?" they asked.

Cindy returned at 10:30 to find Lisa still there, cleaning up again. "You missed your bus!" she exclaimed loudly enough for the two guests to hear her.

"It's no big deal," Lisa insisted. "Besides," Lisa said, pointing at snow flurries out the window, "it's not a great day to hike anyway."

But after Cindy explained to the guests all that Lisa had done for her, they made her an offer. "We're going skiing today. We have an extra ticket. Would you like to come with us?"

When Lisa got in the taxi, Cindy handed her a sealed envelope through the window. Halfway into the mountains, Lisa remembered to open it. Inside were a note and enough money for Lisa to buy a season pass and ski rentals. *Your mountain dream is finally coming true,* said the note. *Did you know that my dream of having a great friend came true as well?*

GO ON →

Student Name _____

6 The following question has two parts. First, answer part A. Then, answer part B.

Part A: Read the sentence from the passage.

One week into her new job, the luck that brought her to Colorado seemed to change.

Which word has **almost the same** meaning as luck as it is used in the sentence?

A effort

B fortune

C opportunity

D surprise

Part B: Which sentence from the passage supports how Lisa's luck changes in part A?

A "Lisa would work Wednesday through Sunday, which sounded perfect."

B "On her days off, she would go hiking in the Rockies."

C "Lisa wouldn't think of leaving her dear friend high and dry, so she toiled around the clock."

D "Just as she was about to leave, two guests came downstairs."

7 The following question has two parts. First, answer part A. Then, answer part B.

Part A: What stops Lisa from exploring the Rocky Mountains sooner?

A She cares about her friend.

B She needs to earn more money.

C She wants to find others to hike with.

D She is confused about how to get there.

GO ON →

Student Name _____

Part B: Which sentence from the passage **best** supports your answer in part A?

A "She was so close to the Rocky Mountains, and yet she couldn't seem to reach them."

B "She joined Happy Trails Hiking Club."

C "Cindy returned at 10:30 to find Lisa still there, cleaning up again."

D "Inside were a note and enough money for Lisa to buy a season pass and ski rentals."

8. Read the sentence from the passage.

Lisa wouldn't think of leaving her dear friend high and dry, so she toiled around the clock.

Draw a line to match each idiom with **one** phrase from the list that most closely matches it.

"high and dry"

"toiled around the clock"

worked every single day with few breaks

was on time for every shift she was assigned

alone and frightened

put out of sight for a while

left alone without any help

GO ON →

Student Name _____

9 Read the sentence from the passage.

All Lisa had to do was walk three blocks to the corner and board a bus by 10 a.m.

Which sentence uses the **same** meaning of the word board as in the sentence?

A   She pays for room and board.

B   He has to board the plane early.

C   They cut the board into many pieces.

D   We will board up the broken window.

10 Explain what the main problem is in "A Mountain Dream" and how it is solved. Use **two** details from the passage to support your answer.

_____

_____

_____

_____

_____

GO ON →

Unit Assessments   Grade 4 • Unit 1   11

Read the passage. Then answer the questions.

Homemade is Best Made

Have you ever wondered about what birthday gift to get a friend? Next time, just walk into your local craft store. There are sparkly beads, silky ribbons, colorful paper, and other fun materials. They are all there to inspire you to create something!

The Perfect Gift

A homemade gift can be whatever you want it to be. If your friend likes turtles, make a gift with a turtle theme. If your friend likes sports, include that in your gift. It's impossible to find a unique gift on the shelves in a store! A gift you buy is never as personal as one you make.

Fun and Easy

Some of the best gifts are easy to make. Most craft stores have pre-made objects to decorate, such as flowerpots or picture frames. Markers, stickers, and colorful tape make decorating a snap. Shopping for the perfect store-made gift is much more difficult. You could spend hours looking in a hundred different stores, but you may never find just the right thing.

Spending Less

A homemade gift usually costs less than something you might buy at a store. For example, a handmade scarf will cost less than a store-bought one. And the handmade scarf will keep your friend just as warm in winter! Why spend more money for an average gift? Make a great one for less money.

Something Special

Any gift you give should come from the heart. A homemade gift is a keepsake your friend will have forever. Don't spend your time and money on an average gift that comes from a store shelf. Instead, have fun crafting, and make the perfect gift for your friends.

GO ON →

Student Name _____

11. Which statement **best** describes the organization of each paragraph?

   A The author contrasts the differences between a homemade gift and a store-bought one.

   B The author compares similarities between a homemade gift and a store-bought one.

   C The author describes a homemade gift and then describes a store-bought one.

   D The author describes a store-bought gift and then compares it to a homemade one.

12. The following question has two parts. First, answer part A. Then, answer part B.

   Part A: Under which heading can the reader find information about deciding what type of homemade gift to make?

   A The Perfect Gift

   B Fun and Easy

   C Spending Less

   D Something Special

   Part B: Which sentence from the passage **best** supports your answer in part A?

   A "A homemade gift can be whatever you want it to be."

   B "Shopping for the perfect store-made gift is much more difficult."

   C "Why spend more money for an average gift?"

   D "A homemade gift is a keepsake your friend will have forever."

GO ON →

Unit Assessments Grade 4 • Unit 1 13

Student Name _____

13 The following question has two parts. First, answer part A. Then, answer part B.

   Part A: What is the main idea of the passage?

   A   Store-bought items make poor gifts for friends.

   B   Homemade gifts are easy to make.

   C   Homemade gifts are better that store-bought ones.

   D   Store-bought and homemade gifts are equally good to give.

   Part B: Which sentence from the passage **best** supports your answer in part A?

   A   "It's impossible to find a unique gift on the shelves in a store!"

   B   "A gift you buy is never as personal as one you make."

   C   "Why spend more money for an average gift?"

   D   "A homemade gift is a keepsake your friend will have forever."

14 Under what heading would the author include details about store-bought gifts selling out when buyers need them most?

   A   The Perfect Gift

   B   Fun and Easy

   C   Spending Less

   D   Something Special

GO ON →

Student Name _____

15 Read the sentence from the passage.

There are sparkly beads, silky ribbons, <u>colorful</u> paper, and other fun materials.

What is the meaning of the word <u>colorful</u>?

A able to be colored

B without color

C the study of color

D having color

UNIT 1

The draft below needs revision. Read the draft. Then answer the questions.

(1) Did you know that the local public library provides books, music, videos, and more for free? (2) That's right. (3) All you have to do is fill out a membership card, but everything in the library is free for you to borrow.

(4) That expensive new book that I want to read is free, as is my favorite summer movie. (5) The library also has computers, study spaces, after-school programs, book clubs, and more. (6) It offers museum passes and host readings by local writers. (7) All this free with your membership card.

(8) The people at the library are helpful, they are very knowledgeable, they help me find great books to read. (9) They also teach me how to do research for my homework. (10) Through the library, I can find tutors to help me with any subject. (11) I can see rare books and historical documents.

(12) I can even volunteer my time and learn about how the library works. (13) All this is free and waiting for you at your local library.

(14) Today's students spend so much of their time and energy wondering where to find the help they need. (15) Stop wasting time in lines and online. (16) Instead, spend more time at the local library. (17) It's free, entertaining, and educational. (18) And which means it's fun.

GO ON →

Student Name _____

16 How can sentence 3 **best** be written?

A All you have to do is fill out a membership card but everything in the library is free for you to borrow.

B All you have to do is fill out a membership card, and everything in the library is free for you to borrow.

C All you have to do is fill out a membership card, but, everything in the library is free for you to borrow.

D All you have to do is fill out a membership card, but everything in the library is free for you to borrow.

17 How can sentence 6 **best** be written?

A It offers museum passes and hosts readings by local writers.

B It offer museum passes and host readings by local writers.

C It offer museum passes and hosts readings by local writers.

D It offers museum passes and host readings by local writers.

18 Which of these is a sentence fragment?

A Sentence 2

B Sentence 4

C Sentence 7

D Sentence 13

GO ON →

Student Name _____

19 How should sentence 8 be written correctly?

  A The people at the library are helpful, and they are very knowledgeable, and they help me find great books to read.

  B The people at the library are helpful. They are very knowledgeable, they help me find great books to read.

  C The people at the library are helpful and knowledgeable, and they help me find great books to read.

  D The people at the library are helpful, they are very knowledgeable, they help me find great books to read.

20 What is the **best** way to combine sentences 17 and 18?

  A It's free, entertaining, and educational, which means it's fun.

  B It's free, entertaining, and educational, and means it's fun.

  C It's free, entertaining, and educational so which means it's fun.

  D It's free, entertaining, and educational and which means it's fun.

Narrative Performance Task

Task:

Your class is learning about how challenges bring out the best in people. Each student must write a story to include in a class book. Before your teacher assigns the story, you do some research and find two articles that provide information about famous people who have overcome challenges.

After you have looked at these sources, you will answer some questions about them. Briefly scan the sources and the three questions that follow. Then, go back and read the sources carefully to gain the information you will need to answer the questions and complete your research.

In Part 2, you will write a story using the information you have read.

Directions for Part 1

You will now look at two sources. You can look at either of the sources as often as you like.

Research Questions:

After looking at the sources, use the rest of the time in Part 1 to answer three questions about them. Your answers to these questions will be scored. Also, your answers will help you think about the information you have read, which should help you write your story. You may refer to the sources when you think it would be helpful. You may also look at your notes.

GO ON →

Source #1: A Show of Courage

The Boy Scouts had been planning the celebration for weeks. Now, the day was here. They were gathered on Bear Mountain in New York for the summer jamboree! The scouts were even getting a visit from Franklin Delano Roosevelt, known as FDR, who was running for vice president of the United States.

As FDR made his rounds at the gathering that day, he shook hands with the scouts and enjoyed a special dinner with them. It was most likely during this visit that a virus would enter his body and change the politician's life forever.

The trip to nearby Campobello Island was supposed to be a vacation. FDR had spent years attending college, getting married and starting a family, and running for office. He was ready to relax. He brought three of his children with him to the family's summer cottage. On that August day, they went sailing, swimming, and hiking. By the time FDR went to bed that evening, he was quite tired. When he awoke in the morning, he was more than tired—he was extremely ill. By the end of the day, pain had spread to his neck and back. He could not move either of his legs.

At first, the doctors were puzzled. Finally, FDR went to a specialist, who told the 39-year-old FDR that he had polio. It was the worst news possible. Roosevelt was running for office! He had important plans! Rather than give up, Roosevelt decided he was not going to let this disease stop him.

FDR and his family worked hard to help him get better. He exercised and soaked in warm mineral springs to improve his muscles. He refused to sit in his wheelchair very often. Instead, he wore heavy braces on his legs to help him walk. Although his ability to move improved some, Roosevelt never was able to walk very far.

This setback might have been enough to defeat many people, but it only strengthened FDR. He went on to become one of the country's most beloved presidents. He was the only president ever elected to four terms in a row. FDR helped the country through some of its most difficult challenges, including the Great Depression of the 1930s and World War II in the 1940s.

Roosevelt also changed countless lives in another way. Each year, on his birthday, a dance was held to raise money for polio research. FDR also started a program called the March of Dimes. It brought in millions of dollars from people all over the country. The money was used to find a cure for the disease. Although a vaccine was not found until ten years after FDR's death, it was his struggle—and his courage— that made a cure possible.

GO ON →

Source #2: A Different Way of Thinking

Temple Grandin is a scientist, author, and professor. She has given lectures to countless people. She has helped make sure that animals are treated kindly. She has also won many awards for her successes. All of this would have been impossible for her family, doctor, and even Grandin herself, to imagine when she was a child.

In 1949, Grandin's mother took her daughter to a doctor. She wanted to find out why her two-year-old was not talking yet. Why didn't she want to be touched? Why did she spend hours watching spinning plates or humming to herself? What was the reason for her screaming temper tantrums? The doctors told Grandin's mother that Temple was autistic. Little was known about autism at that time. The doctors did not believe the young child would ever speak or be able to go to school.

Grandin's mother disagreed. She began reading to her daughter every day. She took her to speech therapy. By age four, Grandin was talking. She went to school, but it was not easy for her. There was so much to see, hear, smell, and touch that Grandin sometimes had panic attacks. Her life changed when she began spending summers at her aunt's cattle ranch. She spent a great deal of time watching the cows. The ranchers put the animals in a squeeze chute to hold them still and calm them while they were getting vaccinated. Grandin was fascinated. She built her own squeeze chute in her bedroom. She crawled into it whenever she felt the need to be held tight and calmed. Today, an updated version of that chute is used in schools and treatment centers for autistic children.

While at the ranch, Grandin also realized something else important. She felt connected to the cattle. She did not think in words like most people. Instead, she thought in pictures. It was as if she could see and feel what the cattle were experiencing. Seeing how the cattle were treated at the ranch gave her many ideas of how farms and ranches could change their methods. Just a few changes would make taking care of cattle easier for the owners and for the animals. Grandin went to college and earned several degrees in animal science. She designed new and different kinds of livestock equipment.

At first, ranchers did not listen to Grandin. They were not used to a woman, especially an autistic woman, telling them they had to make changes. It did not take long, however, before they realized how much better her designs worked for cattle. In 1975, Grandin started her own company.

GO ON →

UNIT 1

Since then, Grandin has written several books about autism, and a movie has been made about her life. She gives talks to people all over the world and answers parents' questions about their autistic children. She reminds them that even though some people's brains see the world differently, they can still invent, create, and make the planet a better place for everyone.

GO ON →

Student Name _____

1. How do paragraphs 1 through 3 add to Source #1? Pick **all** choices that answer the question correctly.

 A They describe the damaging effects of the polio virus.

 B They suggest how FDR may have caught the polio virus.

 C They explain how germs can spread easily among people.

 D They show that the politician will never be the same again.

 E They explain the importance of FDR at that point in history.

 F They show that few medical treatments were available for polio.

 G They explain why the Boy Scouts were excited about the celebration.

2. The sources explain the physical challenges that FDR and Temple Grandin faced. Explain why this information is important to understanding each person's success. Use **one** example from Source #1 and **one** example from Source #2 to support your explanation. For **each** example, include the source title and number.

_____

_____

_____

_____

_____

GO ON →

Unit Assessments   Grade 4 • Unit 1   23

Student Name _____

3 Source #1 and Source #2 discuss how others helped FDR and Temple Grandin deal with their physical challenges. Explain what the sources say about helping others. Use **one** detail from Source #1 and **one** detail from Source #2 to support your explanation. For **each** detail, include the source title or number.

_____

_____

_____

_____

_____

GO ON →

Directions for Part 2

You will now look at your sources; take notes; and plan, draft, revise, and edit your story. First, read your assignment and the information about how your story will be scored. Then begin your work.

Your Assignment:

A visitor comes to your class and describes how she trains companion dogs to help people who have physical challenges. After she is done, your teacher asks you to write a story about a companion dog for either FDR or Temple Grandin. Imagine that the dog is lying quietly on the rug when FDR or Temple Grandin enters the room. In your story, describe how the dog helps FDR or Grandin with his or her physical challenges. The story should be several paragraphs long.

Writers often do research to add realistic details to the setting, characters, and plot in their stories. When writing your story, find ways to use information and details from the sources to improve your story and help you develop your characters, the setting, and the plot. Use details, dialogue, and description where appropriate.

REMEMBER: A well-written story:

- has a clear plot and clear sequence of events
- is well-organized and has a point of view
- uses details from more than one source to support your story
- uses clear language
- follows rules of writing (spelling, punctuation, and grammar usage)

Now begin work on your story. Manage your time carefully so that you can plan, write, revise, and edit the final draft of your story. Write your response on a separate sheet of paper.

Read the passage. Then answer the questions.

How Animals Use Tools

Tools are usually thought of as human inventions. But did you know that animals use tools to solve problems, too?

The chimpanzee, for example, uses grass stems to catch termites. This animal knows where these insects live. It pokes a stem into the termites' nest. Then it waits. Inside the nest, the termites crawl over the stem. The chimpanzee pulls out the termite-covered stem and licks it clean. This is a good meal for a chimpanzee.

This chimpanzee uses a stick as a tool to dig for termites.

Sometimes the chimpanzee has trouble locating water. When this happens, it often uses leaves as a tool. The chimpanzee pushes leaves into places that it cannot reach. The leaves soak up the water from these places. Then the chimpanzee chews on the leaves. Chimps have also been known to use sticks as digging tools.

The woodpecker finch is another animal that uses tools. It uses small sticks to pick insects out of tree bark.

Another animal that uses tools is the sea otter. It uses rocks to crack open shellfish. The otter places the rock on its chest. Then it holds the shellfish in its paws and bangs it against the rock. This cracks the shell open like a treasure chest and allows the otter to eat the creature inside.

The green heron uses bait to catch fish, just as humans use bait on the end of a fishing pole. The heron does this by picking up a small object with its beak. It flies over the water and drops the object onto the surface. Beneath the water, fish see the object and swim toward it. The heron waits for fish to swim close to the surface. Then it swoops down and snaps up the fish.

GO ON →

UNIT 2

Some animals have uses for tools other than gathering food and water. Some use leaves to dab at wounds or to clean things. Some even use twigs as toothpicks. A scientist named Benjamin Beck discovered that crows are very good at solving problems. One unusual crow that lived in Beck's lab ate dry food moistened with a little water. When people forgot to add water to the food, the bird used a cup and added its own water.

The elephant is one of the most intelligent animals. Using its trunk as an arm, the elephant puts grass and branches together. It then uses this tool to swat flies. When needed, this tool can also be used as a back scratcher.

Let's not forget the amazing bottle-nosed dolphins. These remarkable animals twist sea sponges around their snouts. Why? Dolphins hunt the ocean's bottom-dwellers. They use their snouts to turn up sediment and find food. Sometimes they scrape their snouts on sand, rocks, shells, and other objects. Covering their snouts with sponges helps them avoid scrapes, or worse still, stings from poisonous animals.

These are just a few examples of how animals use tools. Scientists are discovering more and more every day. Every time scientists see animals using tools, it makes them rethink their ideas about animal behavior.

GO ON →

Student Name _____

1. The following question has two parts. First, answer part A. Then, answer part B.

   Part A: Which animal uses a tool in **almost the same** way as the chimpanzee?

   A   the woodpecker finch

   B   the sea otter

   C   the green heron

   D   the bottle-nosed dolphin

   Part B: Which sentence from the passage **best** supports your answer in part A?

   A   "First, the otter places the rock on its chest."

   B   "It uses small sticks to pick insects out of tree bark."

   C   "The green heron uses bait to catch fish just as humans use bait on the end of a fishing pole to attract fish."

   D   "Covering their snouts with sponges helps them avoid scrapes, or worse still, stings from poisonous animals."

2. Read the sentence from the passage.

   One <u>unusual</u> crow that lived in Beck's lab ate dry food moistened with a little water.

   The prefix *un-* means "not" or "the opposite of." Which word has **nearly the same** meaning as <u>unusual</u>?

   A   popular

   B   pretty

   C   rare

   D   strong

   GO ON →

Student Name _____

3   Read the sentence from the passage.

   This cracks the shell open like a treasure chest and allows the otter to eat the creature inside.

   What does the simile "like a treasure chest" help the reader understand?

   A   that the otter enjoys eating treasure

   B   that the otter is rewarded with food

   C   that the otter has found buried treasure

   D   that the otter can break into treasure chests

4   The following question has two parts. First, answer part A. Then, answer part B.

   Part A: Which animal uses a tool to protect itself from injury?

   A   the woodpecker finch

   B   the sea otter

   C   the green heron

   D   the bottle-nosed dolphin

   Part B: Which sentence from the passage **best** supports your answer in part A?

   A   "It uses small sticks to pick insects out of tree bark."

   B   "Then it holds the shellfish in its paws and bangs it against the rock."

   C   "Then it swoops down and snaps up the fish."

   D   "Covering their snouts with sponges helps them avoid scrapes, or worse still, stings from poisonous animals."

GO ON →

Student Name _____

5 Explain how the image and caption help the reader better understand the ideas in the passage. Use **two** details from the passage to support your answer.

_____

_____

_____

_____

GO ON →

Unit Assessments — Grade 4 • Unit 2

UNIT 2

Read the passage. Then answer the questions.

The Group Project

Characters
AMIKA
ZOE
NARRATOR
MS. CHAPARRO
LIZZIE

[*Settings*: School cafeteria; Ms. Chaparro's classroom; Amika's house.]

[*Time*: One week in January.]

AMIKA: Have you spoken to the new girl, Lizzie, since she started school this week? She's as quiet as a rabbit eating grass. I haven't even seen her raise her hand to answer questions.

ZOE: No, I haven't, and I haven't seen her in the cafeteria at all. I heard that she stays with Ms. Chaparro in the classroom for lunch.

AMIKA: I'd love to know where she's from, but I feel a little strange just walking up and talking to her.

NARRATOR: The girls return to their classroom and listen while Ms. Chaparro assigns their class a project.

MS. CHAPARRO: For the project, I would like you all to create a three-dimensional representation of one of the scenes from the book we just read. I want you to use your imagination and have fun!

NARRATOR: Amika and Zoe are placed in a group with Lizzie.

AMIKA: Hi, Lizzie. I'm Amika, and this is Zoe. Where are you from?

LIZZIE: [*Timidly.*] Hi. My family just moved from New York because my dad got a job here.

ZOE: New York is far away! I bet it's much different there than it is here.

LIZZIE: [*A little sadly.*] Yes, much different.

GO ON →

[*A brief pause where no one says anything.*]

AMIKA: Well, I've got a terrific idea for what we can do. We can construct the scene from the garden. I've got a big shoebox at home we can use. I'll paint the background on the back of the box. And Zoe, you're always good at making people from pipe cleaners, so why don't you do that?

ZOE: Great! I'm already envisioning some ways I can dress them up.

AMIKA: And Lizzie, why don't you . . . hmmm. Why don't you make some flowers for the garden? Is it possible that you could do that?

LIZZIE: [*Smiling for the first time.*] Oh, yes! I'd love to craft the flowers!

AMIKA: Great. Let's meet at my house on Saturday to put it all together.

NARRATOR: On Saturday, Zoe arrives at Amika's house before Lizzie.

ZOE: Check out the characters I made! Here's the little girl, and here's her mother. [*ZOE demonstrates what she made.*]

AMIKA: Those are really inventive! I wonder what Lizzie has done? She did seem excited about making flowers, so maybe they will be nice.

ZOE: Yeah, I certainly hope so. It must be hard to move so far away from all your friends. I would be miserable if I moved away from you! I think she's been so quiet because she's a little sad.

AMIKA: I think you're right. All the people and things that she's most comfortable with are far away.

NARRATOR: Lizzie arrives at the house toting a big bag.

LIZZIE: I wasn't sure how many flowers you wanted. [*LIZZIE pours a bunch of small paper flowers onto the table.*]

AMIKA: Wow! These will turn our garden into a rainbow!

ZOE: Those are superb, Lizzie! Did you make them yourself?

LIZZIE: [*Lizzie smiles and nods her head.*]

AMIKA: We can put these all over the inside and outside of the box. We're going to have the best project ever!

[*The three girls happily work together on the project.*]

GO ON →

Student Name _____

6 The following question has two parts. First, answer part A. Then, answer part B.

Part A: Read the sentence from the passage.

She's as quiet as a rabbit eating grass.

What does the simile "as quiet as a rabbit eating grass" show about Lizzie?

- A how she looks
- B how she sounds
- C how she smells
- D how she feels

Part B: Which sentence from the passage **best** supports your answer in part A?

- A "'Have you spoken to the new girl, Lizzie, since she started school this week?'"
- B "'I haven't even seen her raise her hand to answer questions.'"
- C "'I'd love to craft the flowers!'"
- D "'I would be miserable if I moved away from you!'"

7 Read the sentence from the passage.

We can construct the scene from the garden.

Which word means the **opposite** of the word construct?

- A destroy
- B claim
- C prepare
- D begin

GO ON →

34 Grade 4 • Unit 2 Unit Assessments

Student Name _____

8 What are the main messages of the play? Pick **two** choices.

  A Everyone must learn to work together to succeed.

  B Looking through another's point of view will help you understand them better.

  C All kinds of people make up the world.

  D You can always be yourself around a true friend.

  E New friendships can ease the pain of a difficult time.

9 How would the play be different if it were written as a story from Lizzie's point of view?

  A It would tell what grade the girls are in.

  B It would include more dialogue.

  C It would explain what Lizzie thinks and feels.

  D It would show why the girls want to talk to Lizzie.

10 Read the sentence from the passage.

These will turn our garden into a rainbow!

What does Amika mean when she says the flowers will turn their garden into "a rainbow"?

  A The flowers will add color to the garden.

  B The flowers are too colorful.

  C A rainbow will appear in the garden.

  D The garden does not have enough color.

GO ON →

Unit Assessments   Grade 4 • Unit 2   35

UNIT 2

Read the poem. Then answer the questions.

Acrobats of the Ocean

The darkened sky recedes at dawn.
Black ocean turns to blue.
A distant sound breaks through the air
As dolphins come into view.

5   Like birds on air they rise and jump,
Light dancing off their skin.
They squeak and chatter through the waves.
They leap, they chase, they spin.

They swim as fast as lightning
10   And rejoin others in their pod.
Jumping high like shooting stars,
They leave observers awed.

These ballet dancers of the sea
Slap tails, butt heads, and play.
15   Their curved mouths always smiling,
They look and swim away.

I'd like to be a dolphin,
Taking care of those I love
While dancing in the ocean air,
20   Sun shining warm above.

GO ON →

Student Name _____

11 Read the lines from the poem.

The darkened sky <u>recedes</u> at dawn.

Black ocean turns to blue.

Which words mean **nearly the opposite** of <u>recedes</u>? Pick **two** choices.

A advances

B remains

C lessens

D hides

E approaches

F gathers

12 The following question has two parts. First, answer part A. Then, answer part B.

Part A: Which sentence **best** states the theme of the poem?

A Dolphins are very happy creatures.

B Dolphins are extremely fast.

C Dolphins move much like birds do.

D Dolphins are the performers of the sea.

Part B: Which line from the poem **best** supports your answer in part A?

A "Like birds on air they rise and jump,"

B "They swim as fast as lightning"

C "They leave observers awed."

D "Their curved mouths always smiling,"

GO ON →

Student Name _____

13 Mark the boxes to show which line **best** supports each point of view. Mark **one** box under **each** point of view.

	Dolphins are fast.	Dolphins are graceful.
"They swim as fast as lightning"	☐	☐
"They leap, they chase, they spin."	☐	☐
"These ballet dancers of the sea"	☐	☐
"While dancing in the ocean air,"	☐	☐

14 What are the poet's reasons for using first-person point of view? Pick **two** choices.

   A to show why the speaker is like a dolphin

   B to express the speaker's wish to be like a dolphin

   C to point out why everyone loves to watch dolphins

   D to show how other animals behave like dolphins

   E to help readers understand why the speaker likes dolphins

GO ON →

Student Name _____

15 The following question has two parts. First, answer part A. Then, answer part B.

Part A: Which sentence provides the **best** summary of the poem?

  A A young person daydreams about what life would be like as a dolphin.

  B An observer admires the beauty and graceful movements of dolphins.

  C A dolphin tries to dance and jump like ballet dancers and acrobats.

  D A group of people watch the dolphins as the creatures play games with each other.

Part B: Which line from the poem **best** supports your answer in part A?

  A "Black ocean turns to blue."

  B "As dolphins come into view."

  C "They swim as fast as lightning"

  D "These ballet dancers of the sea"

GO ON →

The draft below needs revision. Read the draft. Then answer the questions.

(1) When most people think of mammals, they think of land animals, such as Lions. (2) But mammals can also be found living in the water. (3) Examples of marine mammals are whales dolphins, and sea lions. (4) They are similar to land mammals, but they have some major differences that help them survive in a water environment.

(5) First of all there have to be some differences in how land and marine mammals move. (6) Land mammals have strong legs. (7) Their legs allow them to walk and run. (8) Some marine mammals walk, too, like seals and polar bears. (9) However, the most important thing a marine mammal needs to be able to do is to swim, because that is how they catch their food. (10) Whales have very sleek bodies, which help them move through the water easily. (11) They use their tails to swim quickly.

(12) Although land and marine mammals move differently, there are many things about them that are the same. (13) All mammals are warm-blooded. (14) That means that they make their own body heat. (15) Also, all mammals have lungs. (16) Mammals' lungs let them breathe air. (17) Even though marine mammals live in the water and can swim under water for long periods of time, they still need to come to the surface to breathe.

(18) It might seem like whales and lions have nothing in common, but they are more similar than you think. (19) All mammals, no matter where they live, share certain characteristics that make them mammals.

GO ON →

Student Name _____

16 What is the **best** way to write sentence 1?

  A When most poeple think of mammals, they think of land animals, such as Lions.

  B When most people think of Mammals, they think of land animals, such as Lions.

  C When most people think of mammals, they think of land animals, such as lions.

  D When most people think of mammals, they think of land animals, such as Lions.

17 What is the **most** effective revision to make in sentence 3?

  A Examples of marine mammals are whales and dolphins and sea lions.

  B Whales dolphins and sea lions are marine mammal examples.

  C Whales and dolphins, and sea lions are examples of marine mamals.

  D Examples of marine mammals are whales, dolphins, and sea lions.

18 What is the **best** way to write sentence 5?

  A First of all, there have to be some differences in how land and marine mammals move.

  B First of all their have to be some differences in how land and marine mammals move.

  C First of all there have to be some difference's in how land and marine mammals move.

  D First of all there have to be some differences in how land and marine mammals move.

GO ON →

Unit Assessments   Grade 4 • Unit 2   41

Student Name _____

19   What is the **best** way to combine sentences 6 and 7?

   A   Land mammals have strong legs, and their legs allow them to walk and run.

   B   Land mammals have strong legs that allow them to walk and run.

   C   Land mammals have strong legs because they allow them to walk and run.

   D   Land mammals have strong legs, so their legs allow them to walk and run.

20   Which sentence contains a possessive noun?

   A   Sentence 3

   B   Sentence 8

   C   Sentence 10

   D   Sentence 16

Informational Performance Task

Task:

Your class has been learning about animals and how amazing they are. Now your class is going to create a website to share what they have learned. Each student will write something for the website.

Before you decide what animals you will write about, you do some research and find two articles that provide information about how animals communicate, or "talk," to each other. After you have looked at these sources, you will answer some questions about them. Briefly scan the sources and the three questions that follow. Then, go back and read the sources carefully to gain the information you will need to answer the questions and write an informational article for the class website.

In Part 2, you will write your article using information from the two sources.

Directions for Part 1

You will now look at two sources. You can look at either of the sources as often as you like.

Research Questions:

After looking at the sources, use the rest of the time in Part 1 to answer three questions about them. Your answers to these questions will be scored. Also, your answers will help you think about the information you have read, which should help you write your informational article. You may refer to the sources when you think it would be helpful. You may also look at your notes.

GO ON →

Source #1: Can Animals Talk?

People share thoughts and feelings using words. How about animals? Many people think that animals cannot communicate with each other. After all, only humans use words. However, we can also tell each other things without words. We wave our hands to "say" hello and goodbye. We smile, frown, and raise our eyebrows to share how we feel and what we think. Believe it or not, some animals can also tell each other things without using words. Here are a few examples.

Animal Sounds

Animals do not use words or language, but they do make many kinds of sounds. These sounds tell other animals things they need to know. Robins find each other using chirps and songs. Cobras hiss warnings. Blue whales sing low, loud notes to call out to other whales. Scientists now understand that animal songs can vary depending on where each animal lives. So animals can have different accents!

Vervet monkeys warn other monkeys using special sounds. A "cough call" means danger overhead. When the monkeys hear the cough call, they take cover under bushes, look to the skies, and hide from flying predators, like eagles. But Vervet monkeys give a completely different warning sound if danger comes from the ground, such as an oncoming leopard.

Peacocks use their tail feathers to make special sounds, which are so low that human ears cannot hear them! But peahens (female peacocks) can hear them. When they hear tail feathers rustle, they come to see what all the noise is about.

Animal Gestures

Many animals communicate using body language. In Rwanda's Volcanoes National Park, gorillas beat their chests. Are they angry? No, they are happy and letting the other gorillas know how they feel. Dogs let people and other animals know they are happy by wagging their tails. Animals can also send warnings with body language. When cats arch their backs, they are saying, "Stay away!"

Many animals also reach out to express themselves. Chimpanzees help groom their friends. Using their hands, they pat their friends on the back and help keep their fur clean. Grooming leads to cooperation and sharing in the group. This sends the message that they are friends.

GO ON →

Even animals in the seas use touch to tell how they are feeling. Sea otters rub noses with each other. They may even touch noses with other animals like seals and sea lions! This "nosing around" signals play and trust.

So, can animals actually talk? The short answer is "no." Only humans can use words as language. However, animals communicate in many ways. The more we study animals, the more we learn about other methods of communication.

GO ON →

Source #2: Sneaky Animal Signals

Many animals communicate with sights and sounds. Dogs wag their tails. Chickens strut. Pigs grunt. Cats meow. But did you know that some animals can give and receive messages in ways we cannot? Some animals use their powers of touch, taste, and smell to send and receive signals that we can't even sense. How sneaky!

Charged with Feeling

Did you know that some types of fish use electricity to communicate? Some fish send electrical pulses that bounce back to them and tell them where good food is. Other fish, like sharks, for example, can feel the electrical signals of their prey. This way, they can "feel" where their food is. The electrical pulses are not dangerous. They are weak electrical signals that cannot hurt other animals or people. We can't even feel them. Electrical signaling is an ideal type of communication for animals that live in dark, unclear waters.

Chemical Tastes and Smells

Some animals can detect chemical cues that we can't sense at all. Snakes can use their special forked tongues to "taste" the scent of animals in the air. Snakes can tell which chemical cues belong to dangerous animals and which come from animals that would make a good dinner. Snakes have receptors in the roofs of their mouths that help them sense the chemical cues of animals nearby.

Have you ever smelled skunk spray? Skunks spray a stinky odor to protect themselves from predators, like bears, that would otherwise try to eat them! Some animals have scents they use to communicate that we can't detect at all. Have you ever seen a cat rub its head against something? It is marking its territory. Cats have scent glands near their mouths, on their foreheads, and at the base of their tails. They use these organs to mark territory and tell other cats to stay away. Insects communicate with scents, too. Some moths make special chemicals that other moths can sense to find them.

Many animals say things through songs, growls, and whistles. But it is amazing to know that some animals send signals that no one can hear. They can send these signals in daylight or the dark of night. They learn things this way. Animals have a lot to say. We just don't always understand how they say it. Scientists are working to learn more about animals and the incredible signals they use.

GO ON →

Student Name _____

1. Complete the chart to show the source of each detail. Mark **one** box for **each** detail.

	Source #1: Can Animals Talk?	Source #2: Sneaky Animal Signals	Both Source #1 and Source #2
Pulses of electricity can help in finding food.	☐	☐	☐
Senses help animals communicate.	☐	☐	☐
Sounds can warn of danger.	☐	☐	☐

2. Read the sentence from "Sneaky Animal Signals."

But it is amazing to know that some animals send signals that no one can hear.

What details from each source support this sentence? Use **one** detail from **each** source to support your explanation. Be sure to give the source number or title for **each** detail.

_____
_____
_____
_____
_____
_____

GO ON →

Student Name _____

3. Both "Can Animals Talk?" and "Sneaky Animal Signals" give information about how animals send messages.

Explain what you have learned about how animals send messages. Use **one** detail from **each** source to support your explanation. Be sure to give the source number or title for **each** detail.

_____

_____

_____

_____

_____

_____

GO ON →

Directions for Part 2

You will now look at your sources; take notes; and plan, draft, revise, and edit your article for the website. First, read your assignment and the information about how your informational article will be scored. Then begin your work.

Your Assignment:

Your class is creating a website about amazing things animals can do. For your part of the website, you will write an informational article about how animals "talk" to other animals. Your article will be read by students, teachers, parents, and other people who visit the website.

Using information from the two sources, "Can Animals Talk?" and "Sneaky Animal Signals," develop a main idea about how animals communicate. Choose the most important information from more than one source to support your main idea. Then write an informational article several paragraphs long. Clearly organize your article and support your main idea with details from the sources.

Use your own words, except when quoting directly from the sources. Be sure to give the source title when using details from the sources.

REMEMBER: A well-written informational article:

- has a clear main idea
- is well-organized and stays on the topic
- has an introduction and conclusion
- uses transitions
- uses details from the sources to support the main idea
- develops ideas fully
- uses clear language
- follows rules of writing (spelling, punctuation, and grammar usage)

Now begin work on your informational article. Manage your time carefully so that you can plan, write, revise, and edit the final draft of your article. Write your response on a separate sheet of paper.

Read the passage. Then answer the questions.

Critter Crossing

Our teacher, Mr. Singh, had a class project that required us to become involved in something to help our community, so he assigned us to small groups to talk about our ideas. Mr. Singh told us that each group would need to come up with an idea for a project to present to the class. After all of the ideas were presented, the whole class would vote to choose one project we wanted to complete together.

I took one look at my group and felt a black cloud of doom start to gather. First in the group was Max. Actually, Max was my friend, but he was completely obsessed with science, which was not really my thing. One of his birthday presents was a microscope, and he thought it was the most fascinating object in the universe. He could sit at the microscope for hours watching tiny creatures squirm around in a drop of water.

The next member of the group was Iman. All she ever thought about was animals. She even had a lot of pets at home, which would not be a good thing for me. I usually avoided animals because it seemed as though I was allergic to every imaginable kind of animal.

Finally, there was Cally. She was constantly drawing and sketching, and she didn't talk much. She could usually be found sitting somewhere drawing and doodling, which could become annoying if you were hoping to find someone to talk with or do something with after school.

As for me, just get me outdoors! That's all I asked. Whether I was simply bicycling with my friends, walking around town, or playing ball in the park, I was just happy to be outside.

When we sat down to talk about project ideas, Iman started the discussion about what we could do.

"I think our project should be to volunteer at the animal shelter," she said. "It's a great way to contribute to the community, and it will be fun. Of course, that's just one suggestion. I'm going to write down everybody's ideas. But, Theo," she added, staring straight at me, "I really don't think the town needs a new baseball diamond."

Amazing! How did she know what I was going to suggest?

GO ON →

Then Max spoke up. "What about helping wild animals?" he said. Cally started sketching a tiger on her notepad. "I just learned that there is a zoologist at the nature center who we could help. She has been working to save animals on the road by Warner's Woods because the traffic on that road is causing big problems for the wildlife." He glanced at Cally's notepad. "Sorry, Cally," he said. "I'm talking about helping amphibians and reptiles. Not that I wouldn't help tigers if I could!"

"So, what is your suggestion? What are you proposing?" asked Iman.

"Cars and trucks are killing a lot of animals. Spotted salamanders and Blanding's turtles are especially vulnerable because they need to cross the road to get to their nesting grounds. Maybe we could help protect these critters from harm," Max finished.

"We could start a campaign to inform more people about the problem. We could also put signs along the road that would tell people to watch out for turtles and salamanders," suggested Cally.

"Sure," Max agreed. "The zoologist said the spotted salamanders cross the road in huge numbers on the first rainy night in early March. Every year, people from the nature center go out with flashlights and buckets to help them cross safely."

"Maybe some of us could help with that, too," I suggested.

This idea was beginning to sound interesting. We did some research and found pictures of spotted salamanders and Blanding's turtles. Iman immediately fell in love with them, and Cally started designing a 'Critter Crossing' sign.

"What would really help the animals is to have a tunnel under the road just for them," said Max excitedly. "Maybe we could get the town to build one. That would be the best way for the turtles and salamanders to cross safely."

Our group of four agreed that Max's 'Critter Crossing' project was a great idea that could be a big help for our community. Now we would just have to convince the rest of our class that our project was the best!

GO ON →

Student Name _____

1. The following question has two parts. First, answer part A. Then, answer part B.

   Part A: What does Cally **most likely** believe?

   A   Every family should have at least one pet.

   B   Art is often better than words for expressing ideas.

   C   Studying the world around you is often worthwhile.

   D   The school schedule should allow plenty of time for sports.

   Part B: Which detail from the passage **best** supports your answer in part A?

   A   "... he was completely obsessed with science ..."

   B   "... had a lot of pets at home ..."

   C   "... constantly drawing and sketching ..."

   D   "'... the town needs a new baseball diamond.'"

2. The following question has two parts. First, answer part A. Then, answer part B.

   Part A: Read the paragraph from the passage and answer the question.

   "So, what is your suggestion? What are you proposing?" asked Iman.

   Which word is a synonym of proposing?

   A   asking

   B   demanding

   C   guessing

   D   offering

GO ON →

Student Name _____

Part B: Which sentence from the passage **best** supports your answer in part A?

A "'Not that I wouldn't help tigers if I could!'"

B "'Cars and trucks are killing a lot of animals.'"

C "'Spotted salamanders and Blanding's turtles are especially vulnerable because they need to cross the road to get to their nesting grounds.'"

D "'Maybe we could help protect these critters from harm,' Max finished."

3   The following question has two parts. First, answer part A. Then, answer part B.

Part A: Which statement **best** explains how the narrator shows that Iman knows him well?

A Iman is the note taker for the group.

B Iman is friends with the group members.

C Iman is aware of the interests of each group member.

D Iman is certain he will suggest something to do with sports.

Part B: Which sentence from the passage **best** supports your answer in part A?

A "All she ever thought about was animals."

B "'I'm going to write down everybody's ideas.'"

C "How did she know what I was going to suggest?"

D "'What about helping wild animals?' he said."

GO ON →

54   Grade 4 • Unit 3   Unit Assessments

Student Name _____

4 Read the sentences from the passage.

"I just learned there's a zoologist at the nature center who we could help. She has been working to save animals on the road by Warner's Woods because the traffic on that road is causing big problems for the wildlife."

Which word from the passage **best** shows what a zoologist studies?

   A center

   B animals

   C road

   D problems

5 Why would Iman **most likely** think that the Critter Crossing project is a good idea? Use details from the passage to support your answer.

_____

_____

_____

_____

GO ON →

Unit Assessments   Grade 4 • Unit 3   55

Space Exploration is Necessary

Have you ever looked into the sky and wondered about the things in it, such as asteroids, stars, and the sun? There is a universe out there to explore, and we must do so. People say that what is in space is not important to us. That is simply not true. Space holds the answers to many questions, and it is vital that we keep trying to find those answers. There are many reasons why we should explore space.

It's in Our Nature

The astronaut Neil Armstrong said, "From the time of our birth, it is our instinct to explore." As babies, we are always exploring the world around us. We look, touch, and eat things to find out what they are. As we grow older, we want to explore further.

The Creation of Our World

The world would not be what it is today if people never searched beyond where they lived. We know that as long ago as 2300 B.C., humans were exploring lands unknown to them. That is when Egyptians landed on the coast of Africa. The United States was called the "New World" by explorers from Europe who were trying to find lands beyond their own.

Inventions

Inventions, such as the compass, plane, and rocket, all came about to help people explore. The computer was developed to help with space exploration. Think of what other amazing inventions will be created because of space exploration!

Unanswered Questions

Our sun is not the only star in the sky. Scientists think there are ten billion stars in the Milky Way galaxy and that perhaps a million have planets orbiting them. If these planets exist, are they like ours? Do they have life? Only space exploration can answer these questions. What is out in space is important to us, and what we gain in the exploration of it will be invaluable.

GO ON →

Student Name _____

6 Read the sentence from the passage.

Have you ever looked into the sky and wondered about the things in it, such as <u>asteroids</u>, stars, and the sun?

The root of <u>asteroids</u> is the Greek *astro,* meaning "star," and *-oid,* meaning "showing likeness or similarity." What does this suggest <u>asteroids</u> means?

  A small objects in the sky

  B like an astronaut

  C planets

  D stars

7 Read the paragraph from the passage. Underline the sentence that **best** shows that the author thinks space exploration is necessary.

Have you ever looked into the sky and wondered about the things in it, such as asteroids, stars, and the sun? There is a universe out there to explore, and we must do so. People say that what is in space is not important to us. That is simply not true. Space holds the answers to many questions, and it is vital that we keep trying to find those answers. There are many reasons why we should explore space.

8 How does the author organize the passage?

  A by describing the history of space exploration

  B by comparing the positive points and negative points of space exploration

  C by listing the reasons why it is important to explore space

  D by explaining how we can explore space today

GO ON →

Unit Assessments

Student Name _____

9   The following question has two parts. First, answer part A. Then, answer part B.

Part A: Read the sentence from the passage.

What is out in space is important to us, and what we gain in the exploration of it will be invaluable.

Which word means the **opposite** of invaluable as it is used in the sentence?

A   unusual

B   unimportant

C   hidden

D   treasured

Part B: Which word from the sentence **best** supports your answer in part A?

A   space

B   important

C   gain

D   exploration

GO ON →

Student Name _____

10 Complete the chart to show where the new information belongs in the passage. Mark **one** box under **each** heading.

	It's in Our Nature	The Creation of Our World	Inventions	Unanswered Questions
examples of places on Earth that have been explored	☐	☐	☐	☐
examples of things we don't know about	☐	☐	☐	☐
examples of things that have been developed during explorations	☐	☐	☐	☐
examples of ways we explore the world around us	☐	☐	☐	☐

GO ON →

Unit Assessments

A Friend of Nature

Rachel Carson grew up on a farm in Pennsylvania. When Carson was a child, she and her dog, Candy, took long walks through the woods near the farm. They looked at the plants and listened to the sounds of birds and animals. Carson's mother encouraged her daughter's curiosity and love of nature. She helped Carson understand that people were a part of nature.

Her mother did a good job. Years later, Carson wanted to learn more about nature. She took classes in biology. She spent many hours walking through forests and fields studying plant and animal life. Before long, Carson knew she wanted to be a scientist.

Carson's work led her to the Massachusetts coast. She had never before seen the ocean. It was so different from the woods and fields of her Pennsylvania childhood. Carson spent many weeks near tide pools. Tide pools are rocky areas on the edge of the ocean that are filled with seawater. Here she saw unusual creatures she had never observed before. There were starfish in shades of bright red and light pink. Crabs of all sizes rushed to and fro like scurrying insects.

Carson decided to write a book about the sea. She wanted this book to help people discover the great beauty and dazzling variety of life sheltered by the ocean. She also wanted people to know that their lives on land depended on the sea. One of Carson's friends was an artist named Bob Hines. He drew many beautiful pictures for the book she wrote about the sea.

Throughout her life, Carson helped people understand that they should work with nature, not against it. Later, she spoke out against people hurting the environment. She fought against the use of dangerous chemicals that could hurt the environment.

One of her books made people aware of how important it is to protect the environment. In the book called *Silent Spring*, Carson warns that if we do not take better care of the environment, we could lose many animals. The title suggests that,

GO ON →

one day, we might have a spring season in which no birds will be heard because they will have all died. At the time, some people accused Carson of making a mountain out of a molehill. Today, many people feel that this book started the movement to save the environment.

People did not always agree with Rachel Carson. But she fought for what she believed. In time, more and more people came to understand her point of view.

Student Name _____

11 Read the sentences from the passage. Underline the word that helps you understand the meaning of the word coast.

Carson's work led her to the Massachusetts coast. She had never before seen the ocean. It was so different from the woods and fields of her Pennsylvania childhood.

12 Why does the author **most likely** include information about Carson's childhood in the passage? Pick **all** that apply.

A to prove that stories about children are entertaining

B to tell how childhood can influence a person's career

C to show that biographies need to include time in childhood

D to reflect the impact of Carson's mother on Carson's choices

E to make a point about how Carson's mother believed children should be raised

F to show that children should study hard in school so they can pursue their passions

G to show Carson's willingness to study a subject different from what she had grown up with

13 Why does the author consider Carson to be "a friend of nature"?

A because she and her dog Candy would take long walks through the woods

B because she spent many weeks near the tide pools

C because she wrote about how people could affect the environment with their actions

D because her friend Bob Hines drew many beautiful pictures for the book she wrote about the sea

GO ON →

Student Name _____

14 The following question has two parts. First, answer part A. Then, answer part B.

Part A: Read the sentence from the passage.

She took classes in biology.

Which choice would **best** describe what Carson would learn about in a biology class?

A   chemistry

B   microscopes

C   textbooks

D   plants and animals

Part B: Which detail from the passage **best** supports your answer in part A?

A   "... studying plant and animal life ..."

B   "... she wanted to be a scientist ..."

C   "... many beautiful pictures for the book ..."

D   "... the use of dangerous chemicals ..."

GO ON →

Unit Assessments   Grade 4 • Unit 3   63

Student Name _____

15 The following question has two parts. First, answer part A. Then, answer part B.

Part A: What does the author **most likely** believe was important in Carson's books to persuade readers to take better care of the environment?

   A   She had never seen the ocean.

   B   There might one day be no more animals to enjoy.

   C   She made mountains out of molehills.

   D   People should work with nature, not against it.

Part B: Which statement from the passage **best** supports your answer in part A?

   A   "... people accused Carson of making a mountain out of a molehill."

   B   "... Carson helped people understand that they should work with nature ..."

   C   "She had never before seen the ocean."

   D   "... we might have a spring season in which no birds will be heard because they will have all died."

GO ON →

The passage below needs revision. Read the passage. Then answer the questions.

Have you ever ___(1)___ a news announcement? Can you draw? Are you good at making posters? If so, we ___(2)___ your talent on the Publicity Team. We ___(3)___ do it without you!

Last year, a group of fourth graders ___(4)___ a wonderful puppet show. They performed "The Very Hungry Caterpillar" and gave us all a good laugh. We are hoping that some talented actors will plan a performance for this year's festival.

Of course, yummy food is the best part of the Harvest Festival. The pies and spiced cider always ___(5)___ so good! We'll need some great cooks. Please join us as a volunteer and make this year's Fall Harvest Festival the best ever.

GO ON →

Student Name _____

16 Which answer should go in blank (1)?

    A write

    B wrote

    C written

    D writed

17 Which answer should go in blank (2)?

    A use

    B can use

    C have used

    D used to

18 Which answer should go in blank (3)?

    A cann't

    B ca'nt

    C can'

    D can't

GO ON →

Student Name _____

19 Which answer should go in blank (4)?

- **A** were presenting
- **B** presents
- **C** have presented
- **D** presented

20 Which answer should go in blank (5)?

- **A** tasting
- **B** tastes
- **C** taste
- **D** was tasting

Opinion Performance Task

Task:

Your class is creating an online newsletter about how people can make a difference in the world. For your part of the newsletter, you will write an opinion paper about the best ways individuals and companies can help others. Your opinion will be read by students, teachers, parents, and anyone else who reads the school's online newsletter.

After you have reviewed these sources, you will answer some questions about them. Briefly scan the sources and three questions that follow. Then go back and read the sources carefully to gain the information you will need to answer the questions and write an opinion paper.

In Part 2, you will write your opinion paper using information from the two sources.

Directions for Part 1

You will now look at the two sources. You can look at either of the sources as often as you like.

Research Questions:

After reviewing the research sources, use the rest of the time in Part 1 to answer three questions about them. Your answers to these questions will be scored. Also, your answers will help you think about the information you have read and viewed, which should help you write your opinion paper. You may refer to the sources when you think it would be helpful. You may also look at your notes.

GO ON →

Source #1: The Pavement Bookworm

When Philani Dladla walks down the sidewalks of Johannesburg, a city in South Africa, he grabs people's attention. Dressed in a baseball hat, brightly striped dress shirt, and strands of colorful beads, he is like a moving rainbow. What really makes Dladla stand out, however, is the stack of books he is carrying around with him. Those books, and what he does with them, have earned him the nickname "Pavement Bookworm."

Sure, Dladla loves to read. He says it changed his life. His first book was a gift when he was eight years old. He taught himself to read it in English. He read it over and over. As he grew up, the young man struggled with many problems. He began reading self-help books to find some answers and guidance. He discovered that reading helped him become a happier, more knowledgeable person. That passion for books is now what drives him. He spends every day out on the city sidewalks, sharing books with anyone who stops by to look. He finds a busy intersection and sits down. Next, he opens a book, starts to read, and waits for the first person to stop and ask a question.

Dladla is always happy to describe a plot or share a favorite title. He also enjoys having an in-depth discussion about authors, ideas, and publishers. Adults often give Dladla a donation for the book they end up taking along with them. Children, however, are allowed to pick any book he has for free. The Pavement Bookworm loves knowing that he is making a difference in their lives by handing them a book. He believes that kids need to read so they can learn, make wiser decisions as they grow up, and have a better chance of getting hired in the future. Dladla's philosophy is simple. He believes that if you have inspired a single person, you have changed the world.

Philani Dladla's story was first shared with the world in late November 2013. A South African filmmaker named Tebogo Malope spotted Dladla walking along the city streets. He saw him sit down on a bench, put his pile of books down, and start reading. Within a few minutes, people were stopping by to chat.

Malope recorded a video interview with the 25-year-old reader. He posted it online. It did not take long for the story to spread across the globe. Soon, Dladla was being interviewed for a number of radio programs and magazine articles. News spread quickly through Johannesburg, also. Now the bookworm has become a local celebrity. People stop him every day to ask about books. They ask him what they

GO ON →

should read next. Authors have even traveled to visit Dladla. They give him copies of their books to hand out or give away.

Today, Dladla's life is busy with sharing books and organizing reading clubs for young people. The clubs have members from young kids through college students. He hands out books to each one. They read the book. Then they get together to discuss their ideas about what they have read. To make sure that Dladla does not run out of books to sell and give away to others, Malope has been collecting book donations for the Pavement Bookworm. He calls the young man "an amazing ambassador for young people." He wants to do all he can to help a young man whose passion for the written word keeps him going—and sharing.

GO ON →

Source #2: From Box to Backpack

Many people know that cardboard boxes are recyclable and generally helpful to have around. They can be used to mail packages, help a person move, or hold anything from a load of books to a set of dishes. However, it took a nonprofit organization called Aarambh to find out just how amazingly helpful these recycled boxes can be.

Aarambh is based in New Bombay, India. Since its start in 1996, the group has focused on providing educational skills and assistance to children and women throughout India. "Aarambh" is a word that means "beginnings." The organization's main goal is to move "towards a brighter future."

The staff at Aarambh knew that most of the students in Indian schools did not have chairs and desks to sit at or backpacks to carry their books and other supplies. Instead, students sat on the floor with their notebooks spread out in front of them. Naturally, this made it difficult to write clearly and sit comfortably. In addition, students had to carry their school materials home in their arms or inside fragile plastic shopping bags, which were constantly tearing and falling apart. At Aarambh, the workers wanted to improve the situation for the students. The staff developed the Help Desk.

The desks are made out of nothing but recycled cardboard boxes. When folded one direction, the boxes become a sturdy desk with an angled surface for writing and reading. At the end of the day, students can unfold their desks and turn them into carriers to wear on their backs. Flat and rectangular, the carriers look like briefcases. They have a handle that makes it possible to carry them in one hand, or they can also slide onto students' backs.

Aarambh uses the cardboard it gathers from local recycling centers, offices, and businesses. Using free materials helps reduce the cost of manufacturing the desks. In fact, each eco-friendly Help Desk costs less than 20 cents to make.

The process is fairly simple. First, workers carefully trace the outline of the Help Desk onto the flattened out cardboard. Next, they use a laser to cut the sheets of cardboard. Finally, they begin to fold this way and that. Suddenly, a desk appears, as if by magic.

GO ON →

Student Name _____

The Aarambh organization distributes the Help Desks to schools throughout Maharashtra, a state in India's western region. Not too surprisingly, the desks are a big hit with the students. They quickly learn how to fold and unfold the boxes. They have fun switching them from desks to backpacks and back again. Having a surface to write on makes reading, writing, and doing school work far more comfortable. It lessens eye strain and back strain. It also improves overall posture. Best of all, it makes learning easier for the students and encourages them to stay in school.

GO ON →

Student Name _____

1. Both of these sources provide information on how people have made a difference in the world by making it easier for others to learn and further their education. Circle the detail below **each** source that **best** supports this idea.

Source #1

"Those books, and what he does with them, have earned him the nickname 'Pavement Bookworm.'"

"He began reading self-help books to find some answers and guidance."

"He believes that kids need to read so they can learn, make wiser decisions as they grow up, and have a better chance of getting hired in the future."

Source #2

"Best of all, it makes learning easier for the students and encourages them to stay in school."

"Many people know that cardboard boxes are recyclable and generally helpful to have around."

"At the end of the day, students can unfold their desks and turn them into carriers to wear on their backs."

GO ON →

UNIT 3

2. Both "The Pavement Bookworm" and "From Box to Backpack" discuss how to make a difference in the world. What does "The Pavement Bookworm" explain about helping people that "From Box to Backpack" does not? Explain why that information is helpful for the reader. Give **two** details or examples from "The Pavement Bookworm" to support your explanation.

_____
_____
_____
_____
_____
_____
_____

3. "From Box to Backpack" includes information about helping others. Explain how this information would be helpful if it were added to "The Pavement Bookworm." Give **two** details or examples from "From Box to Backpack" to support your explanation.

_____
_____
_____
_____
_____
_____

GO ON →

Directions for Part 2

You will now review your notes and sources and plan, draft, revise, and edit your writing. You may use your notes and go back to the sources. Read your assignment and the information about how your writing will be scored; then begin your work.

Your Assignment:

Your teacher has asked everyone in the class to write an opinion paper that will be used in the school's online newsletter. You are going to write about whether a person can make a bigger or better difference in a community if they are working alone or with a group. Your paper will be read by students, teachers, and parents.

Using both "The Pavement Bookworm" and "From Box to Backpack," develop an opinion about the most effective ways to make a difference in the community. Choose the most important information from both sources to support your opinion. Then write an opinion paper several paragraphs long. Clearly organize your paper and support your opinion with details from the sources. Use your own words, except when quoting directly from the sources. Be sure to give the source title or number when using details from the sources.

REMEMBER: A well-written opinion paper:

- has a clear main idea
- is well-organized and stays on the topic
- has an introduction and conclusion
- uses transitions
- develops ideas clearly
- uses clear language
- follows rules of writing (spelling, punctuation, and grammar usage)

Now begin work on your opinion paper. Manage your time carefully so that you can plan, write, revise, and edit the final draft of your paper. Write your response on a separate sheet of paper.

Read the passage. Then answer the questions.

The Santa Fe Trail

In the 1800s, many trails crossed the American West, and one of these was the Santa Fe Trail. Unlike most trails at the time, it was used mainly for trading. Other trails were used by settlers going to make a new life in the West.

For a while, Spain ruled the area around Santa Fe. The Spanish prohibited trade with the United States. However, after Mexico gained its freedom from Spain, trade between Mexico and the United States began. In 1821, William Becknell made a trip from Missouri to Santa Fe to trade. This was the first of many trips along the trail. The next year, he came back with a wagon train full of goods. At its peak, the trail carried more than two thousand wagons a year.

The trail was about 780 miles long, and it took forty to sixty days to reach Santa Fe from Missouri. The trail followed the Arkansas River and then split into two paths. The first path went with the river to Bent's Fort in Colorado and then turned south through a mountain pass to reach Santa Fe.

The second path went southwest to New Mexico and crossed the desert to Santa Fe. This path was shorter and easier for wagon trains to follow. It did not go through mountains like the first route. The desert was riskier, however, because travelers could run out of water in the desert.

The Santa Fe Trail, 1850

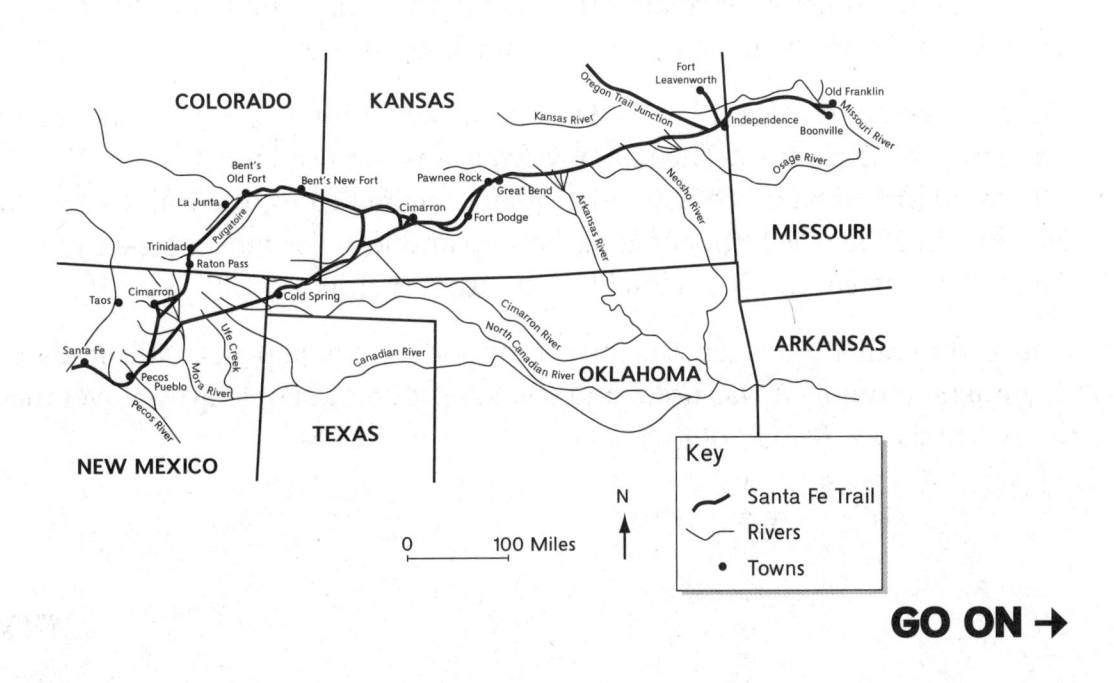

UNIT 5

The Pecos Pueblo

One of the last places the trail passed through was the Pecos Pueblo, which was a group of ruins. Some of the ruins were from an ancient settlement. Others were the remains of old Spanish missions. Stories about these ruins told of lost gold.

Like Santa Fe, the Pecos Pueblo was a trade center. The site was just right for trade because it linked the farming areas of the Rio Grande valley with the hunting areas of the plains. Around A.D. 800, many tribes came to trade, and they brought items such as buffalo hides, shells, pottery, and food.

Because of its value as a trading center, the Pecos Pueblo grew in size. About two thousand people lived at the site between the years 1450 and 1600. They stayed in large buildings that were four or five stories high. They climbed ladders up to each floor, and these ladders could be pulled inside for safety.

The Arrival of the Spanish

In the early 1500s, Spanish explorers came upon the Pecos Pueblo. When the native people met the Spanish, they told them stories about a place called Quivera. This was a city to the east that was supposed to be made of gold. They might have told this story so the Spanish would go look for it and leave them alone. Their idea worked, because the Spanish left to search for the lost city of gold. They never found it.

By the end of the 1500s, more Spanish had arrived. The Pecos Pueblo changed hands a number of times. While the Spanish were in control, they built a church. This church did not survive for long, but another was built later. What is left of this church makes up the most impressive ruins at the site.

As the site kept changing hands, the people living there moved away because they were tired of the unrest. The Santa Fe Trail was not used much after 1880. Once a railroad linked Santa Fe with other major trading cities, the trail was no longer needed. In 1838, the last people packed up and left. For most of the time the Santa Fe Trail was used, the Pecos Pueblo was a desert ruin.

Today, the trail attracts tourists instead of traders. Some people still study the trail to understand how it was used, and a small group of people even travel the trail each year as a way to honor its history.

GO ON →

Student Name _____

1. The following question has two parts. First, answer part A. Then, answer part B.

   Part A: Read the sentence from the passage.

   The desert was <u>riskier</u>, however, because travelers could run out of water in the desert.

   Which word is an antonym of <u>riskier</u>?

   A better

   B easier

   C safer

   D wilder

   Part B: Which detail from the passage **best** supports your answer in part A?

   A "This was the first of many trips along the trail."

   B "It did not go through mountains like the first route."

   C "... because travelers could run out of water in the desert."

   D "... from an ancient settlement."

GO ON →

Unit Assessments Grade 4 • Unit 5 105

Student Name _____

2 Read the sentences from the passage.

The Spanish prohibited trade with the United States. However, after Mexico gained its freedom from Spain, trade between Mexico and the United States began.

Which word has the **opposite** meaning of prohibited as it is used in the passage? Pick **all** that apply.

    A allowed

    B denied

    C ignored

    D outlawed

    E permitted

    F taxed

3 Read the sentence from the passage.

The first path went with the river to Bent's Fort in Colorado and then turned south through a mountain pass to reach Santa Fe.

Which meaning fits pass as it is used in the sentence?

    A narrow route or road

    B throw a ball

    C permission to come and go

    D move past or around something

GO ON →

Student Name _____

4 The following question has two parts. First, answer part A. Then, answer part B.

Part A: Which of these events happened **first** in the history of the Pecos Pueblo?

A   Spaniards began looking for Quivera.

B   William Becknell traveled to Sante Fe.

C   Pecos Pueblo became a trading center.

D   Spanish missionaries came to Pecos Pueblo.

Part B: Which sentence from the passage **best** supports your answer in part A?

A   "The next year, he came back with a wagon train full of goods."

B   "Around A.D. 800, many tribes came to trade, and they brought items such as buffalo hides, shells, pottery, and food."

C   "Their idea worked, because the Spanish left to search for the lost city of gold."

D   "While the Spanish were in control, they built a church."

5 The passage says that the Santa Fe Trail followed the Arkansas River and then split into two paths. Complete the chart to show which problems were had with each path. Mark **one** box next to **each** problem.

	path through the mountains	path through the desert
Less water was available on this path.	☐	☐
Wagon trains had more trouble following this path.	☐	☐
The land was flatter on this path.	☐	☐
There were mountain peaks on this path.	☐	☐

GO ON →

Unit Assessments

UNIT 5

Read the passage. Then answer the questions.

First Day of School

It was the first day of school, and the hallways were buzzing and rattling with the sound of voices shouting back and forth, footsteps tromping, and lockers opening and closing. The sound and activity made it feel like a downtown train station at rush hour. Just to add to the confusion, an announcement came over the speakers that classes would be starting in five minutes. I was grateful I was not a new student this year and already knew where I needed to go for class.

Heading up the stairs, I noticed a girl standing to the side of the hall with Mr. Park, the vice principal. He looked worried, and the girl looked confused. I didn't recognize her—a new student, I thought. Trying to navigate the hallways and stairs was intimidating, especially if you were new.

"Is everything all right, Mr. Park?" I asked.

"Ah, Katherine, hello . . ." replied Mr. Park. He was clearly distracted and kept looking past me towards the school's front doors. "This is Maya Hanson, a new student," he added.

I smiled and said, "Hello there," but Maya did not respond. If anything, she looked more lost than she had a moment earlier.

"Oh, sorry Katherine," said Mr. Park. "Maya is hearing impaired, and we are waiting for Cameron, her interpreter, to get here. He can then help her get settled into Mrs. Randall's class. Apparently, Cameron is running a bit late this morning. I'm afraid that while I can speak English and Spanish, I don't know a single word in sign language."

"Oh!" I exclaimed, suddenly understanding why Maya looked so lost. I tried to imagine what it would be like if I were standing in the hallway of a school where no one spoke my language. It would probably be uncomfortable. Then, I smiled, because I knew something that Mr. Park did not—I knew sign language. Both my Aunt Helena and Uncle Joshua were deaf, so I learned how to sign when I was very small. I could hold entire conversations with my aunt and uncle, and I often interpreted for them at family reunions or events.

GO ON →

"Don't worry, Mr. Park. It turns out every cloud has a silver lining. Now Maya can make a new friend!" Turning to Maya, I quickly signed, "Hello, my name is Katherine, and I can help you until your interpreter arrives."

Maya's face lit up with a huge smile, and she immediately responded, signing, "I am so glad to meet you—and that you know how to sign."

Mr. Park looked quite pleased also, and he immediately asked me if I would be willing to walk with Maya to Mrs. Randall's room.

"We're in the same class," I told Maya, "so I can introduce you to everyone."

When we walked into Mrs. Randall's class, it seemed like every single student was talking, pulling out chairs, and dropping books. Since announcements were still being made, the noise level was incredible. I had an idea about how to lower the volume in the classroom and signed it to Maya, who grinned. She liked the idea as much as I did.

"Mrs. Randall," I said, walking over to our teacher, "I walked to class with Maya, one of the new students. We might have a way to get the class to quiet down."

Mrs. Randall smiled and welcomed Maya to the classroom, and then she stepped back. Maya and I went to the middle of the classroom and began signing to each other. It did not take long for students to notice, and, one by one, they stopped talking to watch us.

"That is so cool," said Steven.

"What are you two saying?" asked LaToya. "Can you show us how to do that too?"

"We can meet Maya and learn about sign language in a few minutes, but first I need to take attendance," said Mrs. Randall firmly. She started to close the door, but at the last minute, a young man slid through the opening and into the classroom.

"I'm Cameron Stewart, Maya's interpreter," he explained.

"Fine," said Mrs. Randall. "I will mark Katherine, Maya, and Cameron as present. Now, let's find out who else is here!"

GO ON →

Student Name _____

6   The following question has two parts. First, answer part A. Then, answer part B.

Part A: Read the sentence from the passage.

The sound and activity made it feel like a downtown train station at rush hour.

What does this sentence suggest about the setting of the story? Pick **two** choices.

   A   There were people waiting in the hallways.

   B   There were stairs leading up from the hallways.

   C   The hallways were very noisy on the first day of school.

   D   There were many students moving through the hallways.

   E   There were announcements over the loudspeaker in the hallways.

Part B: Which detail from the passage **best** supports your answer in part A?

   A   "... hallways were buzzing and rattling with the sound of voices shouting back and forth, footsteps tromping, and lockers opening and closing."

   B   "Just to add to the confusion, an announcement came over the speakers that classes would be starting in five minutes."

   C   "... I was not a new student this year and already knew where I needed to go for class."

   D   "Heading up the stairs, I noticed a girl standing to the side of the hall with Mr. Park, the vice principal."

GO ON →

Student Name _____

7 The following question has two parts. First, answer part A. Then, answer part B.

Part A: Read the sentences from the passage.

"Ah, Katherine, hello . . ." replied Mr. Park. He was clearly distracted and kept looking past me towards the school's front doors.

Which words are antonyms of distracted? Pick **two** choices.

- **A** alarmed
- **B** confused
- **C** focused
- **D** interested
- **E** worried

Part B: Which detail from the passage **best** supports your answer in part A?

- **A** "Trying to navigate the hallways and stairs was intimidating . . ."
- **B** "'Is everything all right, Mr. Park?' I asked."
- **C** ". . . kept looking past me towards the school's front doors."
- **D** ". . . she looked more lost than she had a moment earlier."

GO ON →

Unit Assessments — Grade 4 • Unit 5 — 111

Student Name _____

8 Read the paragraphs from the passage. Underline **two** sentences that indicate what happened to lower the noise level.

When we walked into Mrs. Randall's class, it seemed like every single student was talking, pulling out chairs, and dropping books. Since announcements were still being made, the noise level was incredible. I had an idea about how to lower the volume in the classroom and signed it to Maya, who grinned. She liked the idea as much as I did.

"Mrs. Randall," I said, walking over to our teacher, "I walked to class with Maya, one of the new students. We might have a way to get the class to quiet down."

Mrs. Randall smiled and welcomed Maya to the classroom, and then she stepped back. Maya and I went to the middle of the classroom and began signing to each other. It did not take long for students to notice, and one by one, they stopped talking to watch us.

GO ON →

Student Name _____

9 The following question has two parts. First, answer part A. Then, answer part B.

Part A: Read the sentence from the passage.

"It turns out every cloud has a silver lining."

What is the meaning of the adage "every cloud has a silver lining" as it is used in the passage?

- A It looked like it was going to rain that morning.
- B Every bad thing is made of silver.
- C The clouds outside were silver in color.
- D Good things can come from bad situations.

Part B: Which detail from the passage **best** supports your answer in part A?

- A "Just to add to the confusion . . ."
- B ". . . kept looking past me towards the school's front doors."
- C "If anything, she looked more lost than she had a moment earlier."
- D "'Now Maya can make a new friend!'"

10 What is a problem that the author addresses in "First Day of School"? Support your answer with details from the passage.

_____

_____

_____

_____

GO ON →

Unit Assessments   Grade 4 • Unit 5   113

UNIT 5

Read the passage. Then answer the questions.

An Electrical Circuit

When the battery on your tablet runs out, you need electricity to charge it. To get the electricity into the tablet, you use a charger. When you connect one end of the charger into the device and the other end into a wall outlet, you are creating an electrical circuit through which an electrical current flows.

This may sound very complicated, but it's really simple. You can do a very easy experiment that will let you see how electrical currents work. You will need a battery (the power source), thick tape, a light bulb, and two pieces of wire (the conductors).

First, with an adult's help, cut off about one inch of the rubber coating from each end of the wire. The wires are like a charger cord. They allow electrical charges to flow through them.

Second, tape one end of one wire to the metal part of the light bulb. The light bulb is like your device. It needs electricity to make it work.

Next, connect the other end of the wire to the top of the battery. Get the next piece of wire and tape that to the bottom of the battery. The battery is like the outlet in your wall. It is the power source. At this point of the project, you have a break in the circuit, so the electricity cannot flow to the light bulb. This is called an open circuit.

Finally, you will close the circuit. Touch the last end of wire to the metal part on the light bulb. This closes the circuit and lights the bulb!

Conductors

Conductors are materials that let electricity flow through them. Some good conductors are:

- Copper
- Iron
- Steel

Insulators

Insulators are materials that do not let electricity flow through them. Some good insulators are:

- Rubber
- Wood
- Plastic

GO ON →

Student Name _____

11 According to the passage, what should a person do just **before** taping a piece of wire to the bottom of the battery?

   A   tape one end of a wire to the metal on the light bulb

   B   tape another piece of wire to the top of the battery

   C   touch the battery to the power source

   D   touch the other end of the wire to the metal on the light bulb

12 How does the author organize the information in the passage?

   A   by explaining why electricity makes things work

   B   by listing the steps to take to create an electrical circuit

   C   by convincing the reader to keep their devices charged

   D   by describing devices that use electricity

13 Why did the author **most likely** include the sidebar?

   A   to inform the reader about the materials that do and don't conduct electricity

   B   to describe the different materials that are needed for the project

   C   to tell the reader how to use the materials with electricity

   D   to explain how to follow the steps of the project

GO ON →

Unit Assessments

Student Name _____

14 Complete the chart to show which materials are conductors and which materials are insulators according to the sidebar in the passage. Mark **one** box next to **each** material.

	conductor	insulator
copper	☐	☐
iron	☐	☐
plastic	☐	☐
rubber	☐	☐
steel	☐	☐
wood	☐	☐

15 The following question has two parts. First, answer part A. Then, answer part B.

Part A: According to the passage, which of these tasks should a person do as the **third** step in creating a circuit?

   A   cut off about one inch of the rubber coating from each end of the wire

   B   tape one end of one wire to the metal part of the light bulb

   C   connect the wires to the top and bottom of the battery

   D   touch the last end of wire to the metal part on the light bulb

Part B: Which word from the passage **best** supports your answer in part A?

   A   "First"

   B   "Second"

   C   "Next"

   D   "Finally"

GO ON →

The passage below needs revision. Read the passage. Then answer the questions.

(1) "I just keep my eyes and ears open," Grandma says.

(2) "Don't we all do that?" I ask.

(3) "Most folks just see and hear," she explains, "but I try to look and listen."

(4) Surely that can't be her secret—or is it?

(5) "It is," she says. (6) "You want to know the true history of a small american town? (7) Talk to the people who live there. (8) They're smartest than you think. (9) The old folks can tell you things going back 60 or 70 years before you were born. (10) I'm good at letting folks talk. (11) I got to know our town here. (12) Those town is a very interesting place."

(13) I enjoy listening to my grandma talk. (14) I enjoy it more than anything else.

Student Name _____

16 How can sentence 6 be written correctly?

   A You want to know the true history of a Small american town?

   B You want to know the true history of a small American Town?

   C You want to know the true history of a Small American town?

   D You want to know the true history of a small American town?

17 What is the **best** way to write sentence 8?

   A They're smarter than you think.

   B They're more smart than you think.

   C They're most smarter than you think.

   D They're more smarter than you think.

18 What is the **best** way to combine sentences 10 and 11?

   A I'm good at letting folks talk, but I got to know our town.

   B Because I'm good at letting folks talk, I got to know our town.

   C I'm good at letting folks talk because I got to know our town.

   D Letting folks talk, I'm good at getting to know our town.

GO ON →

Student Name _____

19 What is the **best** way to write sentence 12?

  A This town is a very interesting place.

  B That town is a very interesting place.

  C These town is a very interesting place.

  D Those town is a very interesting place.

20 What is the **best** way to combine sentences 13 and 14?

  A More than anything else, I enjoy listening to my grandma talk.

  B I enjoy listening most than anything else, and my grandma talks.

  C My grandma enjoys listening and talking more than anything else.

  D Most than anything else, I enjoy listening to my grandma talk.

UNIT 5

Informational Performance Task

Task:

Your history class has been learning about the many ways people learn about and remember the past. Your teacher has asked everyone in the class to look up information about the many ways to explore and learn about the past.

For this task, you will be writing an informational article about the ways people learn from the past. You have found three sources on the topic.

After you have reviewed these sources, you will answer some questions about them. Briefly scan the sources and the three questions that follow. Then, go back and read the sources carefully so you will have the information you need to answer the questions and write an informational paper.

In Part 2, you will write an informational paper related to the three sources.

Directions for Part 1

You will now look at the three sources. You can look at these sources as often as you like.

Research Questions:

After reviewing the research sources, use the rest of the time in Part 1 to answer three questions about them. Your answers to these questions will be scored. Also, your answers will help you think about the information you have read and viewed, which should help you write your informational paper. You may refer to the sources when you think it would be helpful. You may also look at your notes.

GO ON →

Source #1: A Moment in Time

Time capsules have been used throughout history. They can be shoeboxes with childhood treasures buried in a backyard. They can also be airtight containers with vital records hidden inside buildings. No matter the scale, the main purpose of time capsules is to help future generations understand the past.

The information in time capsules can tell us what was happening at a point in history. But they can also tell us what people thought was important at that time. Recently, several time capsules have been discovered.

New York, New York

In 1914, New York businessmen buried a chest containing commercial directories and financial reports. These items were meant to celebrate the American Revolution and union of the colonies. Sadly, the chest was forgotten until the 1990s. It was opened in May 2014. The New-York Historical Society, in turn, created its own time capsule. It contains materials meant to capture New York in 2014. These include hand sanitizer, ear buds, a subway card, and popular websites saved on a flash drive.

Boston, Massachusetts

A time capsule from 1901, found in Boston, Massachusetts, was opened in October 2014. The time capsule was sealed inside a lion statue that sits on top of the old statehouse building. Descendants of Samuel Rogers, who made the statue, had recently written a letter telling the city that the capsule was hidden there. The capsule included photos and autographs from government officials at the time. It also included newspaper clippings and political campaign buttons.

Baltimore, Maryland

A 100-year-old time capsule was discovered during the repair of Baltimore's Washington Monument. It contains programs from celebrations at the monument, local newspaper articles, and documents from the 100th anniversary of the Star-Spangled Banner.

GO ON →

UNIT 5

Modern Value

Historian Dr. Yablon says that "disappointment is the most common response to time capsule openings." The contents of time capsules can be interesting, but they do not always lead to new knowledge. And now that technology allows us to save documents and photos so easily, it may not be necessary to save things in a sealed box. In fact, a modern version of a time capsule is being sent to Mars as part of a project by Explore Mars. The project has collected digital images and audio and video messages from millions of people on Earth. The project shows that the value is not just to those who receive the capsule. By choosing what to include, students learn how to decide what is important about their world. They also learn that they are part of a global society.

Time capsules will likely always hold interest to those creating them and finding them. As described above, their value may be debated and may change over time.

GO ON →

Source #2: Digging into the Past

What comes to mind when you think of archaeology? You probably think of dinosaurs and fossils buried in dirt, right? However, this field includes the study of many types of remains or artifacts to learn about life during another time. These can range from cooking tools to weapons to building remains from colonial villages to soil stains left by garbage dumps. Usually, archaeologists dig large holes in areas where societies have been present and remains might be found. Many of these excavation sites are explored for several years.

A wealth of information can be found by studying the remains left during both the ancient and recent past. A few of the main types of archeology are described below.

- **Prehistoric archaeology** provides information about cultures that did not have a written language or were not written about by others. This includes most of what happened more than 3,000 years ago. The only way to learn about these cultures is to unearth and study what they left behind.

- **Historical archaeology** is the study of cultures that existed during recorded history. This includes the study of art, religion, politics, social practices, and more.

- **Underwater archaeology** relates to remains that lie beneath oceans, rivers, and lakes. It includes the study of shipwrecks to understand how they were made and how cities and towns near bodies of water grew and developed.

- **Industrial archaeology** focuses on the history of production. It includes artifacts such as bridges, water, power, canals, and more. These materials show how industry changes over time. It is also a way to study how industry has affected things like travel, street design, and other aspects of life.

Each of these areas of archaeology teaches us about human history and culture. For example, fences at a site relate to how people divided property and shared resources. The location of stone spear points, sometimes found within animal fossils, can indicate where and when hunting took place. We can learn about the

GO ON →

UNIT 5

speed of changes in technology from industrial remains. Also, artifacts from the houses of the employees show how they were treated. Remains can tell us what types of food were eaten, how long people lived, how people spent their days, the size of families, and more.

Archaeology helps us understand where and when people lived on Earth. It also shows why and how they lived. By studying artifacts, we can also learn how information was passed on between civilizations and generations.

GO ON →

Source #3: Family History

More and more people every year are trying to track down their family history. The reasons they do this are varied. Whatever the reason, there are many resources people can use to dive into their pasts.

Keep It Relative

The first step to research your family history is a small one. Many people start by interviewing their own relatives. The oldest ones may have never relied on electronics to remember names and birthdates. They can often remember information about many relatives. Old family books, such as Bibles and family record books, if there are any, can also be good sources. Many people used to record facts about family members in these special books. This could include names, birthdates, marriages, and more. And because family heirlooms were passed down, the information could cover many generations.

Close to Home

Another great resource is the local library. Directories and census counts held by the local library have information on names, birth dates, marriage dates, addresses, and more. For families who have lived in one area for a long time, you may find family names in local newspapers. The library staff, which includes expert researchers, can also direct you to more resources.

Go Global

There are many groups that have taken information, with the help of local libraries and governments, and collected it in one big database. The information from these databases can be accessed online. People also can use websites to research family history. For a fee, these websites can do the legwork for you and research your family tree.

GO ON →

UNIT 5

Why It Matters

There are many reasons why you may want to learn about your family history. Some people want to learn about and connect with their cultural heritage. In doing so, they discover the traditions of where they came from. You may find out that you are related to famous people, or you may find pictures of a great-uncle who has the same nose that you do! You may find that your relatives did something important or discover that your family owns land in a far-off country. You may reconnect with long-lost relatives with whom you share a common history and bond. You also may find more about your family's medical history, which can help you take better care of yourself. Most people find that, by learning about their family, they are also learning about themselves. It often turns out that we all have more in common than we think.

GO ON →

Student Name _____

1   Both Source #1 and Source #2 provide information on what items provide clues to how people lived on a daily basis. Circle **one** detail below **each** source that **best** supports this idea.

Source #1	Source #2
These include hand sanitizer, ear buds, a subway card, and popular websites saved on a flash drive.	Remains can tell us what types of food were eaten, how long people lived, how people spent their days, the sizes of families, and more.
In 1914, New York businessmen buried a chest containing commercial directories and financial reports.	By studying artifacts, we can also learn how information was passed on between civilizations and generations.
No matter the scale, the main purpose of time capsules is to help future generations understand the past.	It includes the study of shipwrecks to understand how they were made and how cities and towns near bodies of water grew and developed.

GO ON →

Unit Assessments   Grade 4 • Unit 5   127

Student Name _____

2 Source #1 and Source #2 discuss how historical clues can help show how people lived in the past. Explain what the sources say about these clues. Use **one** detail from Source #1 and **one** detail from Source #2 to support your explanation. For **each** detail, include the source title or number.

_____
_____
_____
_____
_____

3 Each source explains how to look into the past to learn about it. Explain why this information is important. Use **one** example from Source #2 and **one** example from Source #3 to support your explanation. For **each** example, include the source title and number.

_____
_____
_____
_____
_____

GO ON →

Directions for Part 2

You will now review your notes and sources and plan, draft, revise, and edit your writing. You may use your notes and go back to the sources as often as you need.

Read your assignment and the information about how your writing will be scored; then begin your work.

Your Assignment:

Your teacher is creating a bulletin board display to show what your class has learned about the importance of history. You decide to write an informational article about the many ways people can learn from the past. Your article will be read by students, teachers, and parents.

Using more than one source, develop a main idea about the ways people learn from the past. Write an article that is several paragraphs long in which you explain the ways people can learn about the past. Make sure to have a main idea, organize your article logically, and support your main idea with details from the sources using your own words. Develop your ideas clearly.

REMEMBER: A well-written informational article:

- has a clear main idea
- is well-organized and stays on the topic
- has an introduction and conclusion
- uses transitions
- uses details from the sources to support the main idea
- develops ideas fully
- uses clear language
- follows the rules of writing (spelling, punctuation, and grammar usage)

Now begin work on your informational article. Manage your time carefully so that you can plan, write, revise, and edit the final draft of your article. Write your response on a separate sheet of paper.

Read the passage. Then answer the questions.

Lascaux: A Treasure in the Woods

One night in September 1940, four teenage boys headed for the woods near Montignac, a village in France. They set out with a dog named Robot to look for a cave. As they entered the woods, Robot ran ahead. The boys hiked along until suddenly, they heard Robot barking. Curious, the boys hurried toward Robot to find out what was wrong.

When the boys gathered around what looked like a rabbit hole to look for Robot, the earth collapsed under them. Shocked, they slid fifty feet down and landed in total darkness.

When 14-year-old Jacques Marsal lit their lamp and looked around, he was awed. There were animals painted all over the cave, and the paintings seemed to be moving.

The boys had stumbled into the caves of Lascaux. Inside these caves were some of the most remarkable cave paintings ever found.

Cave Art

These pictures were painted about 17,000 years ago during the Paleolithic Period, which is also called the Stone Age. Nobody knows why these images were painted, but we do know the people who created them were highly skilled.

The Lascaux painters used different colors to create depth and perspective. They also created some stunning effects by spraying paint onto the walls. Scientists suspect they blew paint through hollow bones or from their mouths. With this technique, the colors fade together and create shadows. This is how the animals appear to move.

> **What the Boys Found**
>
> The Lascaux caves contain 850 feet of rooms and tunnels. The painted ceilings are 16 feet high in some places.
>
> There are thousands of images showing humans, objects, and animals, including horses, stags, bison, and wild oxen. They also show a rhino, a bear, and some big cats.
>
> This is amazing because some of these animals do not exist in France today.

The artists at Lascaux painted the animals they saw in real life. However, the Lascaux painters had to invent their own tools using bone and plants, the materials of their world. They made stone lamps and burned animal fat to create light so they could work in the dark caves.

GO ON →

UNIT 6

To reach the ceilings, they created structures to stand on that were attached to the walls. To support these structures, they carved holes in the cave walls and attached poles. The structures were then built across the poles.

Hidden Treasure

Jacques Marsal, one of the boys who found the cave, never lost the feeling of awe. In fact, he devoted his life to protecting the paintings and became Chief Guardian of Lascaux.

When the boys found the caves, the paintings had been hidden for 17,000 years. The air and light in the caves had hardly changed in all those years. After the discovery, the world wanted to see these paintings. However, the people visiting the caves changed the temperature and light, which started to damage the ancient paintings. To protect the paintings and the site, the caves were closed to the public in 1963.

Today, you can see photographs of the cave paintings and visit Lascaux II, which is a replica of two halls of the original cave. Only a few experts can visit the caves to see the paintings firsthand.

The paintings of Lascaux are a window to the past, and a picture is worth a thousand words. These paintings tell us a lot about how people lived during the Stone Age and how they saw the world around them.

GO ON →

Student Name _____

1. The following question has two parts. First, answer part A. Then, answer part B.

   Part A: What is the main idea of the passage?

   A France has many types of animals depicted in art.

   B Cave paintings are an art form that had not been recognized before.

   C The Lascaux caves are a treasure that had been hidden from the world.

   D Jacques Marsal has devoted his life to the Lascaux cave paintings.

   Part B: Which sentence from the passage **best** supports your answer in part A?

   A "Inside these caves were some of the most remarkable cave paintings ever found."

   B "The artists at Lascaux painted the animals they saw in real life."

   C "In fact, he devoted his life to protecting the paintings and became Chief Guardian of Lascaux."

   D "The paintings of Lascaux are a window to the past, and a picture is worth a thousand words."

2. Read the paragraph from the passage. Underline the word that has the **same** connotation as <u>interested</u>.

   One night in September 1940, four teenage boys headed for the woods near Montignac, a village in France. They set out with a dog named Robot to look for a cave. As they entered the woods, Robot ran ahead. The boys hiked along until suddenly, they heard Robot barking. Curious, the boys hurried toward Robot to find out what was wrong.

GO ON →

Student Name _____

3 The following question has two parts. First, answer part A. Then, answer part B.

Part A: Read the sentence from the passage.

However, the people visiting the caves changed the temperature and light, which started to damage the <u>ancient</u> paintings.

Which word has the **same** connotation as <u>ancient</u> as it is used in the passage?

A very old

B old-fashioned

C out-of-date

D worn

Part B: Which sentence from the passage **best** supports your answer in part A?

A "There were animals painted all over the cave, and the paintings seemed to be moving."

B "These pictures were painted about 17,000 years ago during the Paleolithic Period, which is also called the Stone Age."

C "However, the Lascaux painters had to invent their own tools using bone and plants, the materials of their world."

D "The paintings of Lascaux are a window to the past, and a picture is worth a thousand words."

GO ON →

134   Grade 4 • Unit 6   Unit Assessments

Student Name _____

4 Read the sentence from the passage.

After the discovery, the world wanted to see these paintings.

The Latin prefix *dis-* means "opposite of." What is the meaning of the word discovery as it is used in the sentence?

　A　came back

　B　opposite of belief

　C　left a place

　D　something uncovered

5 What information does the sidebar provide for the reader? Pick **two** choices.

　A　the size of the Lascaux caves

　B　where Jacques Marsal is today

　C　where Lascaux is located

　D　how the painters made paint

　E　what is shown in the cave paintings

　F　what tools were used to create shadows

GO ON →

Unit Assessments　　　　　　　　　　　　　　　　　　　　　　　Grade 4 • Unit 6　**135**

Read the passage. Then answer the questions.

A Big New World

As the steam-powered train finally gasped to a halt, Hattie, eager to start her first visit to the city, grabbed her bag. She climbed down to the platform and quickly found her waiting relatives standing not too far from Uncle Harold's brand-new 1915 Model T Ford. As the group walked toward it, Hattie regarded Cousin Lillian's fancy clothes admiringly. However, she noticed that they did seem to make walking rather difficult.

Riding in the automobile was quite an experience as cars elbowed past like people at a crowded party. Because of the noise of so many horns blasting and the smell of the stinky fumes from all those engines, Hattie started to feel ill. When Hattie remarked on all this, Lillian was puzzled.

"This is not a large amount of traffic," she said. "Are there many cars where you live?" She couldn't believe it when Hattie said that there were not many cars and that the small number of cars they had didn't all go out on the road at the same moment.

After a slow trip across town, they arrived at a tall brick house with a red front door. Inside, Aunt Mabel exclaimed, "Better late than never!" upon seeing them. Then she briskly steered Hattie into the warm front room, where Hattie was very happy to accept the welcoming arms of a big, soft armchair. She tried answering her aunt's questions but could not help yawning. Seeing that Hattie was completely exhausted, Aunt Mabel suggested an early bedtime and led her upstairs to show her around.

Hattie was amazed by the washroom upstairs. At home, the family took baths in a tub they carried into the kitchen and used water from the well that they heated on the woodstove. Because this was such a long process, they did not take baths often. Here at her relatives' home were both hot and cold water, coming right into the house, so you didn't have to preheat the water or carry anything!

During the night, Hattie woke to the sound of something clanking and hissing in her room. She cried out, frightened, and Aunt Mabel and Uncle Harold quickly appeared to learn what was wrong.

GO ON →

"That noise is only the steam in the radiator," her uncle said, pointing to a large metal object along the wall. "It's noisy. All these new houses heat with steam instead of fireplaces."

As her aunt and uncle walked back to their room, Hattie heard Lillian across the hall softly asking, "Hasn't she ever seen a radiator before?"

In the morning, Hattie stood in the kitchen doorway watching as the maid, Nora, cooked breakfast. The kitchen was very new and modern-looking, and the sink had hot and cold faucets just like the washroom. The white monster squatting in the corner turned out to be a refrigerator. The stove had metal coils that heated up when you turned some handles, and Nora said it ran on electricity, not wood. Hattie had heard about these inventions but had never seen them.

"Would you like some toast?" asked Nora. Mmmmmm! Hattie nodded. Nora attached the bread to a metal box with wire racks on the outside, plugged the metal box into the wall, and the wire racks started to glow.

"When one side gets brown, turn this knob to toast the other side," she said. "Watch carefully so it doesn't burn."

At home they made toast over the fire on a toasting fork, so Hattie knew about watching toast. How was this machine an improvement?

Hattie soon discovered that her relatives owned all of the latest gadgets. They also took pride in showing off their up-to-date city, and Lillian was amused when Hattie exclaimed about the modern marvels on every corner. To Lillian, all these devices were ordinary. She didn't understand that Hattie was seeing a new world—strange, exciting, and a little bit scary.

When Hattie returned to her home, she told her parents about all she had witnessed. "Some of those new gadgets and machines do make life easier. Sometimes, however, they're not any easier, or they even cause problems."

Hattie's father replied, "The challenge is figuring out when a new way of doing something is really better. Now, how about some old-fashioned toast?"

GO ON →

Student Name _____

6 Read the sentence from the passage.

As the steam-powered train finally gasped to a halt, Hattie, eager to start her first visit to the city, grabbed her bag.

What does the personification of the train as it "gasped to a halt" suggest that the train was doing?

   A   The train was making noises as it stopped.

   B   The train was going very fast using its engine.

   C   The train whistle was blowing to let people know it had arrived.

   D   The train was making awful fumes that made the passengers sick.

7 Which **two** sentences from the passage are examples of imagery?

   A   "Riding in the automobile was quite an experience as cars elbowed past like people at a crowded party."

   B   "Hattie soon discovered that her relatives owned all of the latest gadgets."

   C   "Hattie was amazed by the washroom upstairs."

   D   "However, she noticed that they did seem to make walking rather difficult."

   E   "The white monster squatting in the corner turned out to be a refrigerator."

GO ON →

Student Name _____

8 The following question has two parts. First, answer part A. Then, answer part B.

Part A: Read the sentence from the passage.

Here at her relatives' home were both hot and cold water, coming right into the house, so you didn't have to preheat the water or carry anything!

What does the word preheat mean as it is used in the sentence?

- A to heat water fully
- B to heat water after
- C to heat water again
- D to heat water before

Part B: Which detail from the passage **best** supports your answer in part A?

- A "... carried into the kitchen ..."
- B "... water from the well ..."
- C "... on the woodstove."
- D "... take baths often."

9 The following question has two parts. First, answer part A. Then, answer part B.

Part A: Which sentence **best** describes the lesson Hattie learns in the passage?

- A Family members enjoy having visitors.
- B Traveling by train is better than by car.
- C New inventions make life easier and harder.
- D Life in a city is nearly the same as in a small town.

GO ON →

Unit Assessments   Grade 4 • Unit 6   139

Student Name _____

Part B: Which sentence from the passage **best** supports your answer in part A?

A "Because of the noise of so many horns blasting and the smell of the stinky fumes from all those engines, Hattie started to feel ill."

B "Seeing that Hattie was completely exhausted, Aunt Mabel suggested an early bedtime and led her upstairs to show her around."

C "Hattie's father replied, 'The challenge is figuring out when a new way of doing something is really better.'"

D "She cried out, frightened, and Aunt Mabel and Uncle Harold quickly appeared to learn what was wrong."

10   Read the paragraph from the passage.

After a slow trip across town, they arrived at a tall brick house with a red front door. Inside, Aunt Mabel exclaimed, "Better late than never!" upon seeing them. Then she briskly steered Hattie into the warm front room, where Hattie was very happy to accept the welcoming arms of a big, soft armchair. She tried answering her aunt's questions but could not help yawning. Seeing that Hattie was completely exhausted, Aunt Mabel suggested an early bedtime and led her upstairs to show her around.

How does the author's use of imagery and personification add to the passage? Use details from the paragraph to support your answer.

_____

_____

_____

_____

GO ON →

Read the passage. Then answer the questions.

The Wayfarer
by Stephen Crane

The Wayfarer,

Perceiving[1] the pathway to truth,

Was struck with astonishment.

It was thickly grown with weeds.

5   "Ha," he said,

"I see that none has passed here

In a long time."

Later he saw that each weed

Was a singular[2] knife.

10 "Well," he mumbled at last,

"Doubtless there are other roads."

---

[1] **Perceiving**—finding or realizing
[2] **singular**—single

"The Wayfarer" by Stephen Crane from *An American Anthology, 1787–1900*. Houghton Mifflin, 1900.

GO ON →

Student Name _____

11   Which sentence **best** states the main message of the poem?

   A   The path to truth is difficult, so it is often skipped.

   B   There is really only one path in life.

   C   New paths are not always meant to be taken.

   D   We all have our own paths to follow.

   Part B: Which detail from the poem **best** supports your answer in part A?

   A   "Perceiving the pathway to truth,"

   B   "Was struck with astonishment."

   C   "'I see that none has passed here In a long time.'"

   D   "'Well,' he mumbled at last,"

12   Why does the speaker in the poem compare the weeds to knives?

   A   to show that the path to truth does not really exist

   B   to show that the path to truth is difficult to travel

   C   to show that the path to truth is full of lies

   D   to show that the path to truth does not end

GO ON →

Student Name _____

13   The main ideas of the poem are listed along the top of the chart. Complete the chart to match the statements from the poem with each main idea. Mark **one** box next to **each** statement.

	People choose to believe what they want.	Few people seek out the truth.	The truth can be painful or difficult to bear.
"the pathway to truth . . . was thickly grown with weeds."	☐	☐	☐
". . . each weed was a singular knife."	☐	☐	☐
"'Doubtless there are other roads.'"	☐	☐	☐

14   What do the paths and roads in the poem represent?

   A   ways of living

   B   trails the speaker likes walking

   C   ways to weed the lawn

   D   ways to walk to the store

15   Read the lines from the poem.

Later he saw that each weed
Was a singular knife.

The speaker uses weeds and knives as metaphors to describe the scene. What is this an example of?

   A   synonym

   B   imagery

   C   personification

   D   simile

GO ON →

Unit Assessments   Grade 4 • Unit 6   143

UNIT 6

The passage below needs revision. Read the passage. Then answer the questions.

(1) The morning chill was still in the air on December 17, 1903 in Kitty Hawk, North Carolina. (2) Orville Wright's airplane wheels had lifted off the ground! (3) The flight had lasted only 12 seconds, but the Wright brothers had just changed how people traveled forever.

(4) Orville's plane, called Flyer, was built by him and his brother, Wilbur. (5) They had been working on a plane with a motor for years. (6) No one had never built a plane with a motor that could be steered, so they had to figure out how to do it on their own.

(7) They decided they were ready to try out Flyer on December 14, and they tossed a coin to see which brother would get to go first. (8) Wilbur won the toss, but when they got to the beach, there wasn't enough wind. (9) Wilbur ended up gliding Flyer down from a hill.

(10) Three days later, they were ready to try again and went back to Kitty Hawk beach. (11) The weather was cold and, most important, windy. (12) Since Wilbur "flew" the plane last, it was Orville's turn. (13) They turned on the engine and propellers. (14) Orville lay down flat on his stomach. (15) Then, Wilbur let go of the rope holding the plane in place, and Flyer started to move a track they had set up. (16) After about 40 feet, the plane left the ground and headed into the air! (17) The plane they had built had worked good. (18) Even though the plane only flew for 120 feet, the Wright brothers and Flyer let the world know that it could be done.

GO ON →

Student Name _____

16 Which of these sentences would **best** follow and support sentence 1?

   A Because of this, Orville Wright's airplane wheels had lifted off the ground!

   B That was when Orville Wright's airplane wheels had lifted off the ground!

   C Importantly, Orville Wright's airplane wheels had lifted off the ground!

   D In other words, Orville Wright's airplane wheels had lifted off the ground!

17 Which sentence contains a double negative that needs to be corrected?

   A Sentence 3

   B Sentence 6

   C Sentence 8

   D Sentence 18

18 How can sentence 14 **best** be written for the most detail?

   A Orville lay down flat on his stomach and was ready to go.

   B Then Orville lay down flat on his stomach.

   C To fly the plane, Orville had to lay down flat on his stomach.

   D Orville lay down flat on his stomach in the middle of the bottom wing.

GO ON →

Unit Assessments Grade 4 • Unit 6 145

Student Name _____

19   How can sentence 15 **best** be written?

   A   Then, Wilbur let go of the rope holds the plane in place, and Flyer started to move a track they had set up.

   B   Then, Wilbur let go of the rope holding the plane in place and Flyer started to move a track they had set up.

   C   Then, Wilbur let go of the rope holding the plane in place, and Flyer started to move along a track they had set up.

   D   Then, Wilbur let go of the rope holding the plane in place, and Flyer started to move a track they had set up.

20   How can sentence 17 **best** be written?

   A   It they had built had worked good.

   B   The plane they had builded had worked good.

   C   The plane they had built had worked well.

   D   The plane they had built had worked good,

Opinion Performance Task

UNIT 6

Task:

Your class has an upcoming field trip to a local wind farm. To prepare for this trip, you have been learning about how wind power can generate electricity. Your teacher has asked everyone in the class to look up information on the differences between renewable and non-renewable energy sources. You have found two sources on the topic.

After you have reviewed these sources, you will answer some questions about them. Briefly scan the sources and the three questions that follow. Then, go back and read the sources carefully so you will have the information you need to answer the questions and write an opinion paper.

In Part 2, you will write an opinion paper using information from the two sources.

Directions for Part 1

You will now look at the two sources. You can look at either of the sources as often as you like.

Research Questions:

After reviewing the research sources, use the rest of the time in Part 1 to answer three questions about them. Your answers to these questions will be scored. Also, your answers will help you think about the information you have read and viewed, which should help you write your opinion paper. You may refer to the sources when you think it would be helpful. You may also look at your notes.

GO ON →

Unit Assessments   Grade 4 • Unit 6   **147**

UNIT 6

Source #1: Energy Efficiency and Conservation

Energy is another word for power. Energy efficiency means using energy wisely. By saving energy, we are saving money. We are buying less fuel, saving resources, and creating less pollution.

Efficiency

Each job that needs power uses a different amount of energy. These jobs range from lighting a room to operating a video game system to powering a piece of equipment at a factory. As you can imagine, there are millions of different pieces of equipment and machines that use electricity and other types of energy.

Many types of fuels used to produce electricity have become more costly and difficult to find. For this reason, people are trying to make machines that use less energy. For example, new types of light bulbs use less energy than older types of light bulbs to produce the same amount of light. Energy efficiency is so important that the United States Department of Energy now has an Office of Energy Efficiency and Renewable Energy. This office teaches people about using energy wisely.

The United States Environmental Protection Agency (USEPA) also has a program called Energy Star®. Through the program, appliances that are more efficient than others are labeled with an Energy Star® sticker. People buying appliances can use the sticker to help them find more efficient appliances.

GO ON →

Conservation

Energy conservation means using less energy. It is closely related to energy efficiency. There are things everyone can do to conserve energy. A few examples are:

- Turning off lights when you leave a room
- Using sunlight instead of electric lights whenever you can
- Closing windows and doors if the heat or air conditioning is on to keep that air inside the building
- Deciding what you want to eat before opening the refrigerator door so that the cool air has less time to escape

Many government agencies and companies have tools to help people calculate how much energy they are using. People can then change their habits or appliances to save electricity and power.

Always Improving

The biggest use of electricity in homes is for air conditioning. Next is lighting and large appliances, like ovens. Lighting is the biggest use of electricity in schools, stores, and other public buildings. It is easy to see that increased energy efficiency can help save a lot of electricity. Companies now look for ways to make appliances and other machines more efficient. Because saving energy means saving money and creating less pollution, people have many reasons to be efficient and use power wisely.

GO ON →

Source #2: Renewable Energy Sources: How They Are Used in the United States

The following information is part of a presentation on how renewable energy sources are used in the United States.

Renewable Energy Sources

How They Are Used in the United States

Renewable Energy

- Renewable energy sources are not consumed or used up.
- Renewable energy sources can be used to provide heat and make electricity.

GO ON →

Renewable Energy

The five main types of renewable energy are:

- Biomass
- Hydropower
- Geothermal
- Wind
- Solar

Biomass

- Biomass is material from plants and animals.
- Examples: wood, wood waste, crops, trash, animal manure, human sewage, and biofuels (ethanol, biodiesel)
- When biomass is burned, energy is released as heat.
- Gas that is released from biomass can also be used as energy.
- In 2017, biomass provided about **1.6%** of the energy used in the United States to make electricity.

GO ON →

UNIT 6

Hydropower

- Hydropower captures energy from moving water.
- The first hydroelectric power plant in the United States opened in 1882.
- Hydropower is the largest renewable resource for making electricity in the United States.
- In 2017, hydropower provided about **6.5%** of the energy used in the United States for electricity generation.

Geothermal

- The word *geothermal* comes from the Greek words *geo,* meaning earth, and *therme,* meaning heat.
- Geothermal energy comes from heat—like steam or hot water—from the earth.
- There are more geothermal power plants in the western United States and Hawaii, where geothermal energy sources are closer to Earth's surface.
- In 2017, geothermal sources provided about **0.4%** of the energy used in the United States for making electricity.

GO ON →

Wind

- Wind turbines, which are like windmills, use blades to collect energy from the wind.

- In recent years, wind has been the fastest growing source of electricity in the United States.

- By 2011, 36 different states had large wind turbines.

- In 2017, wind sources provided about **6.3%** of the energy used in the United States for electricity generation.

Solar

- Solar energy is energy from the sun.

- Solar energy can provide electricity to individual houses or create electricity at a power plant for large areas.

- Solar energy could be a huge source of power. If just 4% of the world's desert areas were covered with panels to collect solar energy, the entire world could be supplied with energy.

- In 2017, solar energy provided about **1.3%** of the energy used in the United States for making electricity.

GO ON →

UNIT 6

Use of Renewable Energy in the United States

- Wood has been used as a fuel for thousands of years.

- Fossil fuels—like coal, petroleum, and natural gas—replaced wood as a primary energy source over time.

- As fossil fuels become harder and more expensive to find, renewable energy sources have become more popular.

- Today, more than half of renewable energy is used for producing electricity.

- In 2017, **17%** of electricity was generated from renewable energy sources. More than half of this was from hydropower.

Some Benefits of Renewable Energy

- Generally, renewable energy sources produce less air pollution than non-renewable energy sources (fossil fuels). This includes the pollution that causes climate change.

- While fossil fuels become more expensive and difficult to find, renewable energy sources will never run out.

- By burning trash, less waste is placed into overcrowded landfills.

GO ON →

Some Drawbacks to Renewable Energy

- Dams used for hydropower may obstruct fish migration and change these habitats.

- Some people feel that wind turbines ruin the view and are too noisy.

- A large area of land is required to capture enough solar energy to provide large amounts of electricity.

- While renewable energy sources do not run out, their supply is not constant.

Student Name _____

1. Both sources provide information about the problem with using traditional fuel sources. Circle the detail below **each** source that **best** supports this idea.

Source #1	Source #2
Companies now look for ways to make appliances and other machines more efficient.	As fossil fuels become harder and more expensive to find, renewable energy sources have become more popular.
Many types of fuel used to produce electricity have become more costly and difficult to find.	Fossil fuels—like coal, petroleum, and natural gas—replaced wood as a primary energy source over time.

2. Both Source #1 and Source #2 discuss energy sources. What does Source #2 explain about energy sources that Source #1 does not? Explain why that information is helpful for the reader. Give **two** details or examples from Source #2 to support your explanation.

_____

_____

_____

_____

_____

GO ON →

Student Name _____

3 Each source explains the concept of energy resources. Explain why knowing where energy comes from and how it is used is important. Use **one** example from Source #1 and **one** example from Source #2 to support your explanation. For **each** example, include the source title and number.

_____

_____

_____

_____

_____

GO ON →

UNIT 6

Directions for Part 2

You will now review your notes and sources and plan, draft, revise, and edit your writing. You may use your notes and go back to the sources as often as you need.

Read your assignment and the information about how your writing will be scored; then begin your work.

Your Assignment:

A few days before your class trip to the wind farm, your teacher asks all students in your class to write their opinion about how the school should reduce its energy usage. These opinion papers will be read by your classmates, your teacher, and the principal.

Your assignment is to use information from the sources to write an opinion paper about the best ways the school can reduce the amount of energy it uses. Make sure you clearly state your opinion with reasons and details from the sources. Develop your ideas clearly and use your own words, except when quoting directly from the sources. Be sure to give the source title or number for the details or facts you use.

REMEMBER: A well-written opinion paper:

- has a clear opinion
- is well-organized and stays on the topic
- has an introduction and conclusion
- uses transitions
- uses details or facts from more than one source to support your opinion
- develops ideas clearly
- uses clear language
- follows rules of writing (spelling, punctuation, and grammar usage)

Now begin work on your opinion paper. Manage your time carefully so that you can plan, write, revise, and edit the final draft of your opinion paper. Write your response on a separate sheet of paper.

Unit 1 Answer Key

Student Name: _____

Question	Correct Answer	Content Focus	Complexity
1A	B	Main Idea and Key Details	DOK 2
1B	D	Main Idea and Key Details/Text Evidence	DOK 2
2A	D	Text Structure: Compare and Contrast	DOK 2
2B	D	Text Structure: Compare and Contrast/Text Evidence	DOK 2
3	A	Context Clues: Multiple-Meaning Words	DOK 2
4A	C	Context Clues: Multiple-Meaning Words	DOK 2
4B	B	Context Clues: Multiple-Meaning Words/Text Evidence	DOK 2
5	see below	Text Structure: Cause and Effect	DOK 2
6A	B	Context Clues: Synonyms	DOK 2
6B	C	Context Clues: Synonyms/Text Evidence	DOK 2
7A	A	Character, Setting, Plot: Problem and Solution	DOK 2
7B	C	Character, Setting, Plot: Problem and Solution/Text Evidence	DOK 2
8	see below	Figurative Language: Idioms	DOK 2
9	B	Context Clues: Multiple-Meaning Words	DOK 2
10	see below	Character, Setting, Plot: Problem and Solution	DOK 3
11	A	Text Structure: Compare and Contrast	DOK 2
12A	A	Heads and Diagrams or Graphs	DOK 1
12B	A	Heads and Diagrams or Graphs/ Text Evidence	DOK 2
13A	C	Main Idea and Key Details	DOK 2
13B	B	Main Idea and Key Details/ Text Evidence	DOK 2
14	B	Text Features: Heads and Diagrams or Graphs	DOK 2
15	D	Suffixes: -ful	DOK 1
16	B	Coordinating Conjunctions	DOK 1
17	A	Compound Subjects and Predicates	DOK 1

Unit Assessments

Unit 1 Answer Key   Student Name: _____

Question	Correct Answer	Content Focus	Complexity
18	C	Sentence Fragments	DOK 1
19	C	Correcting Run-Ons	DOK 1
20	A	Punctuate Complex Sentences	DOK 1

Comprehension 1A, 1B, 2A, 2B, 5, 7A, 7B, 10, 11, 12A, 12B, 13A, 13B, 14	/18	%
Vocabulary 3, 4A, 4B, 6A, 6B, 8, 9, 15	/12	%
English Language Conventions 16, 17, 18, 19, 20	/5	%
Total Unit 1 Assessment Score	/35	%

5   Students should match the following:
- People wanted faster ways to send information out West.
  The Pony Express was created to send letters in 25 days.
- Morse overheard people discussing whether it was possible to send messages along a wire.
  The working model of a telegraph was invented.
- Telegraph wires connected the East Coast to the West Coast.
  News was able to travel at lightning speed.

8   Students should match the following:
- high and dry: left alone without any help
- toiled around the clock: worked every single day with few breaks

10   **2-point response:** The problem is that Lisa is working so hard for her friend Cindy that she does not get the chance to go to the mountains, which is the reason she moved to Colorado in the first place. The problem is finally solved when Cindy sees how much Lisa is giving up. She arranges for Lisa to go skiing and gives her all the money she needs to get a pass and rent her ski equipment.

Unit 1 Answer Key   Student Name: _____

Narrative Performance Task			
Question	Answer	Complexity	Score
1	B, D, E	DOK 3	/1
2	see below	DOK 3	/2
3	see below	DOK 3	/2
Story	see below	DOK 4	/4 [P/O] /4 [D/E] /2 [C]
Total Score			/15

2 **2-point response:** The information about the physical challenges that Roosevelt and Grandin faced helps the reader understand how impressive it is that Roosevelt and Grandin achieved so much. Source #1 tells how, despite needing heavy braces on his legs to walk and being unable to walk far, Roosevelt was elected to four terms as U.S. President and helped the country through the Great Depression and World War II. Source #2 tells how, despite her trouble learning to talk and going to school, Grandin earned several degrees and now gives talks about autism to people around the world.

3 **2-point response:** The descriptions of how other people helped Roosevelt and Grandin deal with their challenges show that people can make the world a better place by trying to help people. Source #1 says that Roosevelt and his family worked hard to help him get better. His doctors figured out what was wrong with him, and people all over the country donated money to try to find a cure. Finally, a vaccine was found. Source #2 tells how Grandin's mother read to her every day and took her to speech therapy to teach her to talk. If her mother had accepted what the doctors said and given up trying to teach her to talk, Grandin might never have been able to go to school or eventually write books.

Unit 1 Answer Key

Student Name: _____

10-point anchor paper: As I lay on the warm rug, listening lazily to the fire crackling in the fireplace, I enjoyed the warmth that filled the room. I was just about to drift off to sleep when Prez rolled into the room. I called him Prez, but just about everyone else, except his family, called him Mr. President. His full name was Franklin Delano Roosevelt, and he was my master and the President of the United States.

I was a service dog, and I came to live with him after he became sick with polio. It was a terrible illness that had no cure. I spent a long time being trained especially for him. It was my job to help him in any way that I could. I brought him things, alerted him to dangerous situations, or just sat by him and let him pet my long, golden fur. He seemed to enjoy the petting most of all. I did too.

Quickly, I jumped up to greet him. I stood in front of him, wagging my tail to let him know how happy I was to see him.

"Sammy," he asked me, "are you enjoying the warmth of that fire on this cold December day?" He rolled closer to feel the warmth himself.

Knowing the routine, I grabbed the newspaper from the table and brought it to him. After I set it in his lap, I licked his hand and nudged my nose under it, wanting a good pet.

"You are such a good dog, Sammy. Always right there when I need you." Rubbing the backs of my ears in appreciation, Prez looked intently at the opened newspaper. He scanned the dark shapes on the pages. I never quite understood why he did this, but he seemed to think it was important. He often got angry at whatever he saw.

After a long pause, he sighed. "Oh, why don't they listen? Things will never get better without everyone helping!"

Dropping the paper in his lap, he looked at me seriously. "Sammy, go get Mrs. Roosevelt."

Immediately I sprinted out the door and down the hall to find Mrs. Roosevelt. When I found her, she was just finishing with breakfast. Excited to complete my job, I bounded into the room and gave a short bark to get her attention.

"Sammy?" she asked. But then, understanding why I was there, she replied, "I am coming." She hurried down the hall to Prez's office.

"Is everything all right, dear?" she asked, even before fully entering the room.

"Oh, yes," he answered, sounding frustrated. "I didn't mean to alarm you. I just need to go meet with my staff. I think I might have an idea that will help our troops fighting in the war. Sammy, grab my case and follow me! We are going to work!"

Grabbing his case, I followed him. I knew that I would need to be right by his side, helping him all day. I would help him by holding open doors, bringing him important files, and even bringing him the case that held the braces he sometimes wore on his legs. I was his companion dog, and I was there to help him however I could.

Unit 1 Rationales

1A

A is incorrect because there are not enough details to support this as the main idea of the passage.

B is correct because the passage is mainly about the ways communication has improved since 1850.

C is incorrect because there are not enough details to support this as the main idea of the passage.

D is incorrect because there are not enough details to support this as the main idea of the passage.

1B

A is incorrect because this sentence is a detail that does not support the main idea of the passage.

B is incorrect because this sentence is a detail that does not support the main idea of the passage.

C is incorrect because this sentence is a detail that does not support the main idea of the passage.

D is correct because it refers to the many ways communication has improved since 1850.

2A

A is incorrect because the passage makes no mention of the price of pony rentals.

B is incorrect because people could not prefer the telegraph over the Pony Express if it wasn't invented yet.

C is incorrect because it is a reason for why people would prefer the Pony Express.

D is correct because the speed of communication was why people preferred the telegraph.

2B

A is incorrect because it refers to the cheapest way to travel, not communicate.

B is incorrect because it states what the people wanted, not what they preferred to use.

C is incorrect because it refers to the invention of the telegraph, not what people preferred to use.

D is correct because it implies that the speed of the telegraph for communication put the Pony Express out of business.

3

A is correct because "to allow to go through" is how the word is used in the sentence.

B is incorrect because this is not the meaning of the word as it is used in the sentence.

C is incorrect because this is not the meaning of the word as it is used in the sentence.

D is incorrect because this is not the meaning of the word as it is used in the sentence.

4A

A is incorrect because this is not the meaning of the word as it is used in the sentence.

B is incorrect because this is not the meaning of the word as it is used in the sentence.

C is correct because "to go toward" is how the word "head" is used in the sentence.

D is incorrect because this is not the meaning of the word as it is used in the sentence.

4B

A is incorrect because the sentence does not help the reader determine the meaning of the word "head."

B is correct because it indicates that Americans were traveling.

C is incorrect because the sentence does not help the reader determine the meaning of the word "head."

D is incorrect because the sentence does not help the reader determine the meaning of the word "head."

5

"People wanted faster ways to send information out West" should match to "The Pony Express was created to send letters in 25 days" because the first event caused the second.

"Morse overheard people discussing whether it was possible to send messages along a wire" should match to "The working model of a telegraph was invented" because the first event caused the second.

"Telegraph wires connected the East Coast to the West Coast" should match to "News was able to travel at lightning speed" because the first event caused the second.

6A

A is incorrect because "luck" does not mean "effort" in this sentence.

B is correct because "luck" means "fortune" in this sentence.

C is incorrect because "luck" does not mean "opportunity" in this sentence.

D is incorrect because "luck" does not mean "surprise" in this sentence.

6B

A is incorrect because it refers to Lisa's work schedule, not how her luck changes.

B is incorrect because it refers to how Lisa would spend her days off, not how her luck changes.

C is correct because Lisa had to toil around the clock after her friend got injured, changing her luck from good to bad.

D is incorrect because it refers to events that happen later in the story.

7A

A is correct because Lisa stays behind to pick up extra work while her friend is injured.

B is incorrect because earning money does not keep Lisa from exploring the mountains sooner.

C is incorrect because finding hiking partners does not keep Lisa from exploring the mountains sooner.

D is incorrect because being confused does not keep Lisa from exploring the mountains sooner.

7B

A is incorrect because it simply states that Lisa could not get to the mountains.

B is incorrect because it does not detail how circumstances kept her from exploring the mountains.

C is correct because it shows how Lisa missed the bus to the mountains to help her friend.

D is incorrect because it does not detail how circumstances kept her from exploring the mountains.

8

"High and dry" matches to "left alone without any help" and "toiled around the clock" matches to "worked every single day with few breaks" because these are the meanings of the idioms.

9

A is incorrect because it is not the meaning of the word "board" as it is used in the sentence.

B is correct because "board" means "to get on" in the sentence.

C is incorrect because it is not the meaning of the word "board" as it is used in the sentence.

D is incorrect because it is not the meaning of the word "board" as it is used in the sentence.

10

See answer key for sample response.

11

A is correct because each paragraph addresses the strengths of a homemade gift followed by the failures of a store-bought one.

B is incorrect because the paragraphs do not address the strengths of a store-bought gift but do describe the strengths of a homemade gift.

C is incorrect because the author does not describe any particular homemade or store-bought gift in every paragraph.

D is incorrect because the author first addresses homemade gifts and then store-bought ones in each paragraph.

12A

A is correct because this section discusses how a homemade gift is unique and fits the needs of the person for whom you are making it.

B is incorrect because this section discusses decorating a homemade gift after you have decided what to make.

C is incorrect because this section discusses how homemade gifts are cost-effective.

D is incorrect because this section discusses why homemade gifts are thoughtful gifts.

12B

A is correct because it introduces the topic of what sort of homemade gift the reader can make.

B is incorrect because it refers to shopping for homemade gifts, not making a homemade gift.

C is incorrect because it refers to buying a gift from the store.

D is incorrect because it refers to the recipient keeping a gift, not what sort of gift to make.

13A

A is incorrect because the statement addresses only half of the subject of the passage.

B is incorrect because the statement fails to address the remaining strengths of homemade gifts and the weaknesses of store-bought ones.

C is correct because the statement includes both points the author makes in the passage.

D is incorrect because the passage does not describe both types of gifts as equally good.

13B

A is incorrect because it only refers to the cons of a store-bought gift.

B is correct because it states how a store-bought gift is not as good as a homemade gift.

C is incorrect because it only refers to the cons of a store-bought gift.

D is incorrect because it only refers to the benefit of a homemade gift.

14

A is incorrect because this section points out how store-bought gifts are not unique and personal.

B is correct because this section discusses how buyers often have difficulty finding store-bought gifts.

C is incorrect because this section discusses how store-bought gifts cost more money than homemade gifts.

D is incorrect because this section discusses how store-bought gifts are average compared to homemade gifts.

15

A is incorrect because the suffix "-ful" does not mean "able."

B is incorrect because the suffix "-ful" does not mean "without."

C is incorrect because the suffix "-ful" does not mean "the study of."

D is correct because the suffix "-ful" means "full of" or "having."

16

A is incorrect because the comma is needed to separate the two clauses.

B is correct because "and" is the correct coordinating conjunction for the sentence.

C is incorrect because the comma is correctly placed before the coordinating conjunction.

D is incorrect because the sentence includes an error in the choice of coordinating conjunction.

17

A is correct because the singular subject "It" agrees with its singular compound verbs "offers" and "hosts."

B is incorrect because the verbs "offer" and "host" should be singular to agree with their subject, "It."

C is incorrect because the verb "offer" should be singular to agree with its subject, "It."

D is incorrect because the subject "It" must agree with its compound verbs "offers" and "hosts."

18

A is incorrect because it is not a sentence fragment.

B is incorrect because it is not a sentence fragment.

C is correct because it is a sentence fragment.

D is incorrect because it is not a sentence fragment.

19

A is incorrect because adding the conjunction "and" does not solve the run-on issue.

B is incorrect because making the first clause its own sentence solves the first run-on issue, but not the second.

C is correct because deleting "they are very" and adding "and" creates a single sentence that is not a run-on.

D is incorrect because the sentence is a run-on created by the incorrect linking of three independent clauses.

20

A is correct because a comma and relative pronoun connects a dependent clause to an independent clause, making a correct complex sentence.

B is incorrect because the comma and conjunction must be followed by an independent clause.

C is incorrect because "so which means" incorrectly connects the two clauses.

D is incorrect because the relative pronoun that creates a dependent clause must be preceded by a comma and not "and."

Unit Assessments   Grade 4 • Unit 1 Answer Key

Unit 2 Answer Key   Student Name: _____

Question	Correct Answer	Content Focus	Complexity
1A	A	Main Idea and Key Details	DOK 3
1B	B	Main Idea and Key Details/Text Evidence	DOK 3
2	C	Prefixes	DOK 2
3	B	Figurative Language: Similes and Metaphors	DOK 2
4A	D	Main Idea and Key Details	DOK 2
4B	D	Main Idea and Key Details/Text Evidence	DOK 2
5	see below	Text Features: Photographs with Captions	DOK 3
6A	B	Figurative Language: Similes and Metaphors	DOK 2
6B	B	Figurative Language: Similes and Metaphors/Text Evidence	DOK 2
7	A	Context Clues: Antonyms	DOK 2
8	B, E	Theme	DOK 3
9	C	Point of View	DOK 3
10	A	Figurative Language: Similes and Metaphors	DOK 2
11	see below	Context Clues: Antonyms	DOK 2
12A	D	Theme	DOK 3
12B	C	Theme/Text Evidence	DOK 3
13	see below	Point of View	DOK 3
14	B, E	Point of View	DOK 3
15A	B	Theme	DOK 3
15B	D	Theme/Text Evidence	DOK 3
16	C	Common and Proper Nouns	DOK 1
17	D	Commas in a Series	DOK 2
18	A	Phrases and Interjections	DOK 1
19	B	Combining Sentences	DOK 2
20	D	Possessive Nouns	DOK 1

168   Grade 4 • Unit 2 Answer Key   Unit Assessments

Unit 2 Answer Key   Student Name: _____

Comprehension 1A, 1B, 4A, 4B, 5, 8, 9, 12A, 12B, 13, 14, 15A, 15B	/18	%
Vocabulary 2, 3, 6A, 6B, 7, 10, 11	/12	%
English Language Conventions 16, 17, 18, 19, 20	/5	%
Total Unit 2 Assessment Score	/35	%

5   **2-point response:** This image shows a chimpanzee using a stick as a tool. It is an example of what the passage describes in words, and it helps readers visualize the action.

11   Students should match the following:
- recedes: advances, approaches
- rejoin: separate, leave

13   Students should match the following:
- Dolphins are fast: "They swim as fast as lightning," "They leap, they chase, they spin."
- Dolphins are graceful: "These ballet dancers of the sea," "While dancing in the ocean air,"

Unit 2 Answer Key   Student Name: _____

Informational Performance Task			
Question	Answer	Complexity	Score
1	see below	DOK 3	/1
2	see below	DOK 3	/2
3	see below	DOK 3	/2
Informational Article	see below	DOK 4	/4 [P/O] /4 [E/E] /2 [C]
Total Score			/15

1. Students should match the following statements:
   - Source #1: Can Animals Talk?: Sounds can warn of danger.
   - Source #2: Sneaky Animal Signals: Pulses of electricity can help in finding food.
   - Both Source #1 and Source #2: Senses help animals communicate.

2. **2-point response:** Some animals send signals that no one can hear. In Source #2, we learned that sharks detect their prey by feeling the electrical signals. They can "feel" where their food is. In Source #1, we learned that male peacocks communicate by rustling their feathers to attract a mate. The sound they make is so low that a human is unable to hear it.

3. **2-point response:** Both sources discuss how animals can communicate by sending special messages. In Source #2, we learned that cats have special glands on their foreheads near their mouths and at the base of their tail to mark their territory with a special scent. In Source #1, we learned that Vervet monkeys use special sounds, including one that sounds like a cough, to warn other monkeys that dangerous predators are near.

10-point anchor paper: Have you ever wondered how animals "talk" to each other? Do they communicate like we do? Many scientists have spent time studying animals and have discovered that animals do not communicate using language like humans do. Humans communicate using speech or writing. If they want to tell a friend something, they use language to communicate. However, animals can "talk" to each other in other ways. They communicate using methods such as sight, smell, touch, and even body language.

One way is sound. According to Source #1, animals use sounds to tell other animals things they need to know. One animal, the Vervet monkey, uses a special sound like a cough to warn other monkeys in their group of danger from above. The "cough call" tells the other monkeys to hide under a bush because a predator, like an eagle, is in the sky. The monkeys make a different noise when others are in danger from a predator on the ground.

Unit 2 Rationales

1A

A is correct because the woodpecker finch uses a tool in almost the same way as the chimpanzee.

B is incorrect because the sea otter does not use a tool in the same way as the chimpanzee.

C is incorrect because the green heron does not use a tool in the same way as the chimpanzee.

D is incorrect because the bottle-nosed dolphin does not use a tool in the same way as the chimpanzee.

1B

A is incorrect because the sentence does not detail how the animal uses a tool like a chimpanzee.

B is correct because the sentence details how the animal uses a tool like a chimpanzee.

C is incorrect because this sentence does not detail how the animal uses a tool like a chimpanzee.

D is incorrect because this sentence does not detail how the animal uses a tool like a chimpanzee.

2

A is incorrect because it is not the meaning of the word "unusual" as it is used in the sentence.

B is incorrect because it is not the meaning of the word "unusual" as it is used in the sentence.

C is correct because "unusual" means "rare" in the sentence.

D is incorrect because it is not the meaning of the word "unusual" as it is used in the sentence.

3

A is incorrect because it is not the meaning of the simile.

B is correct because the simile "like a treasure chest" means that the otter is rewarded with food when it cracks the shell open.

C is incorrect because it is not the meaning of the simile.

D is incorrect because it is not the meaning of the simile.

4A

A is incorrect because it is never stated that this animal uses a tool to protect itself from injury.

B is incorrect because it is never stated that this animal uses a tool to protect itself from injury.

C is incorrect because it is never stated that this animal uses a tool to protect itself from injury.

D is correct because the bottle-nosed dolphin uses a sponge to protect itself from injury.

4B

A is incorrect because this sentence does not detail how a dolphin uses a tool to protect itself from injury.

B is incorrect because this sentence does not detail how a dolphin uses a tool to protect itself from injury.

C is incorrect because this sentence does not detail how a dolphin uses a tool to protect itself from injury.

D is correct because this sentence details how a dolphin uses a tool to protect itself from injury.

5

See answer key for sample response.

6A

A is incorrect because the simile describes how Lizzie sounds in school, not how she looks.

B is correct because the simile describes how Lizzie sounds in school.

C is incorrect because the simile does not describe how Lizzie smells.

D is incorrect because the simile does not describe how Lizzie feels.

6B

A is incorrect because the sentence does not refer to how Lizzie sounds in school.

B is correct because the sentence refers to how Lizzie never speaks up in school.

C is incorrect because the sentence does not refer to how Lizzie sounds in school.

D is incorrect because the sentence does not refer to how Lizzie sounds in school.

7

A is correct because "destroy" and "construct" are antonyms; "construct" means "build," and "destroy" means "break down."

B is incorrect because "claim" and "construct" do not have opposite meanings; "claim" means "demand," and "construct" means "build."

C is incorrect because "prepare" and "construct" do not have opposite meanings; "prepare" means "get ready," and "construct" means "build."

D is incorrect because "begin" and "construct" do not have opposite meanings; "begin" means "start," and "construct" means "build."

8

A is incorrect because the girls do not have any trouble learning how to work together in the play.

B is correct because Amika and Zoe realize how difficult it would be if one of them were to move away from each other, so they understand Lizzie's sadness better.

C is incorrect because it's hard to know how different the girls are in the play based on the details provided.

D is incorrect because Lizzie has just met Amika and Zoe, so the message of the play would not be related to true friends.

E is correct because Lizzie smiles and appears to start to feel better about her move from New York once Amika and Zoe welcome her.

9

A is incorrect because a story told from Lizzie's point of view would not necessarily include details about what grade the girls are in.

B is incorrect because the play is primarily dialogue, so it is unlikely that a story would include more.

C is correct because a story told from the first-person point of view often includes details about the main character's thoughts and feelings.

D is incorrect because a story told from Lizzie's point of view would reveal more about Lizzie and not the other girls.

10

A is correct because the flowers will add color to the garden, like a rainbow adds color to the sky.

B is incorrect because there is no indication that the flowers are too colorful.

C is incorrect because there is no indication that a rainbow will appear in the garden.

D is incorrect because there is no indication that the garden does not have enough color.

11

"Recedes" matches to "advances" and "approaches" because they are antonyms.
"Rejoin" matches to "separate" and "leave" because they are antonyms.

12A

A is incorrect because this is not the theme of the poem.

B is incorrect because this is not the theme of the poem.

C is incorrect because this is not the theme of the poem.

D is correct because the theme of the poem is how dolphins are the performers of the sea.

12B

A is incorrect because it refers to how dolphins move, not that they are performing for anyone.

B is incorrect because it refers to how dolphins move, not that they are performing for anyone.

C is correct because it refers to how the audience is delighted to watch the dolphins perform.

D is incorrect because it refers to how dolphins smile, not that they are performing for anyone.

13

"Dolphins are fast" matches to "They swim as fast as lightning" and "They leap, they chase, they spin" because these lines from the poem describe how the dolphins move quickly in the water.

"Dolphins are graceful" matches to "These ballet dancers of the sea" and "While dancing in the ocean air," because these lines from the poem describe how the dolphins move gracefully.

14

A is incorrect because the speaker never states that they are like a dolphin.

B is correct because the first-person point of view allows the reader to know that the speaker wishes to be a dolphin.

C is incorrect because this could be stated in first or third-person point of view.

D is incorrect because the speaker never mentions other animals.

E is correct because the first-person point of view allows the reader to know why the speaker likes dolphins.

15A

A is incorrect because this information is only covered in the final stanza.

B is correct because the majority of the poem talks about the speaker admiring how dolphins move.

C is incorrect because this information is only covered in one stanza of the poem.

D is incorrect because this information is only covered in one stanza of the poem.

15B

A is incorrect because it is describing the ocean, not how dolphins are graceful.

B is incorrect because it is describing how they come into view, not how dolphins are graceful.

C is incorrect because it only describes one way the dolphins move gracefully, not that they are graceful.

D is correct because it describes dolphins as ballet dancers, who are known for their graceful movements.

16

A is incorrect because "people" is the correct spelling.

B is incorrect because "mammals" is not a proper noun.

C is correct because "lions" is not a proper noun.

D is incorrect because the "L" in "lions" should be lowercase.

17

A is incorrect because it does not include commas to separate the items in the series.

B is incorrect because it does not include commas to separate the items in the series.

C is incorrect because it does not include commas to separate all the items in the series.

D is correct because it includes commas to separate each item in the series.

18

A is correct because there should be a comma after the introductory phrase "First of all."

B is incorrect because "there" is the correct spelling for this sentence.

C is incorrect because "differences" is not possessive.

D is incorrect because there should be a comma after the introductory phrase "First of all."

19

A is incorrect because it is not the best way to combine the sentences.

B is correct because it is the best way to combine the sentences.

C is incorrect because it is not the best way to combine the sentences.

D is incorrect because it is not the best way to combine the sentences.

20

A is incorrect because it does not contain a possessive noun.

B is incorrect because it does not contain a possessive noun.

C is incorrect because it does not contain a possessive noun.

D is correct because it contains a possessive noun.

Unit 3 Answer Key

Student Name: _____

Question	Correct Answer	Content Focus	Complexity
1A	B	Point of View	DOK 2
1B	C	Point of View/Text Evidence	DOK 2
2A	D	Context Clues: Synonyms and Antonyms	DOK 2
2B	D	Context Clues: Synonyms and Antonyms/Text Evidence	DOK 2
3A	D	Point of View	DOK 2
3B	C	Point of View/Text Evidence	DOK 2
4	B	Context Clues: Definitions and Restatements	DOK 2
5	see below	Point of View	DOK 3
6	A	Greek Roots	DOK 1
7	see below	Author's Point of View	DOK 3
8	C	Author's Point of View	DOK 2
9A	B	Context Clues: Synonyms and Antonyms	DOK 2
9B	B	Context Clues: Synonyms and Antonyms/Text Evidence	DOK 2
10	see below	Author's Point of View	DOK 3
11	see below	Context Clues: Definitions and Restatements	DOK 2
12	B, D, G	Author's Point of View	DOK 3
13	C	Author's Point of View	DOK 3
14A	D	Context Clues: Paragraph Clues	DOK 1
14B	A	Context Clues: Paragraph Clues/ Text Evidence	DOK 1
15A	B	Author's Point of View	DOK 2
15B	D	Author's Point of View/Text Evidence	DOK 2
16	C	Irregular Verbs	DOK 1
17	B	Main and Helping Verbs	DOK 1

Unit 3 Answer Key   Student Name: _____

Question	Correct Answer	Content Focus	Complexity
18	D	Punctuation in Contractions	DOK 1
19	D	Subject-Verb Agreement	DOK 1
20	C	Verb Tenses	DOK 1

Comprehension 1A, 1B, 3A, 3B, 5, 7, 8, 10, 12, 13, 15A, 15B	/18	%
Vocabulary 2A, 2B, 4, 6, 9A, 9B, 11, 14A, 14B	/12	%
English Language Conventions 16, 17, 18, 19, 20	/5	%
Total Unit 3 Assessment Score	/35	%

5   **2-point response:** The Critter Crossing project is a great project for Iman because she is really interested in animals. She has lots of pets at home and is accused by Theo of thinking of animals all the time.

7   Students should underline the following sentence: Space holds the answers to many questions, and it is vital that we keep trying to find those answers.

10 Students should match the following:
  • It's in Our Nature: Examples of ways we explore the world around us
  • The Creation of Our World: Examples of places on Earth that have been explored
  • Inventions: Examples of things that have been developed during explorations
  • Unanswered Questions: Examples of things we don't know about

11 Students should underline the following word: ocean

Unit 3 Answer Key   Student Name: _____

Opinion Performance Task			
Question	Answer	Complexity	Score
1	see below	DOK 3	/1
2	see below	DOK 3	/2
3	see below	DOK 3	/2
Opinion Paper	see below	DOK 4	/4 [P/O] /4 [E/E] /2 [C]
Total Score			/15

1. Students should circle the following statements:
   - Source #1: "He believes that kids need to read so they can learn, make wiser decisions as they grow up, and have a better chance of getting hired in the future."
   - Source #2: "Best of all, it makes learning easier for the students and encourages them to stay in school."

2. **2-point response:** "The Pavement Bookworm" shows how you can make a difference all by yourself rather than having to be part of a company or organization. It focuses on the difference an individual can make within the community. It also points out that how Dladla helps people he comes into contact with face to face, and of all ages, rather than specific ages and groups. That is inspiring for others who would like to make a difference but are not sure how to do so.

3. **2-point response:** "From Box to Backpack" includes information on how to help a greater number of people at a time, rather than the individual who may or may not stop by to chat. In addition, it shows how the idea can be shared with others in order to have a greater impact on the world. This information would be great if added to "The Pavement Bookworm," as it would show how Dladla's idea could ripple out and affect more people.

10-point anchor paper: I believe that Philani Dladla is performing an excellent community service by handing out and selling books to people. However, I feel that the employees at Aarambh are making a bigger impact on their community.

Instead of reaching the people who may stop by and chat, as with Dladla, the Indian company is making products that are being sent out to much larger groups of people. They are not waiting for someone to approach them for help or suggestions, as with the Pavement Bookworm, but are instead producing portable desks and sending them to classrooms. In addition, the work they do to make these cardboard desks can be shared with others and spread out across the world to wherever the desks may help.

Aarambh is not only helping get people interested in reading but actually helping students study all the different subjects they learn in school. It is improving students' lives by providing cardboard desks so they can write comfortably. The desks are eco-friendly, cost less than 20 cents each to make, and can be easily carried as a backpack. Students like them and stay in school longer because the desks relieve eye strain and back strain. So Aarambh is living up to its name, which means "beginnings," and its goal of moving "towards a brighter future."

Based on what I learned here, it is my opinion that working with a group of people is the most effective way to make a difference in the world. Since you have more money, help, and materials, you can reach more people and cause a bigger ripple to spread across the world.

Unit 3 Rationales

1A

A is incorrect because Cally shows no interest in having pets in the passage.

B is correct because Cally loves drawing, so she likely thinks art is the best way to express ideas.

C is incorrect because Cally does not express this idea in the passage.

D is incorrect because Cally does not express this idea in the passage.

1B

A is incorrect because this detail refers to Max, not Cally.

B is incorrect because this detail refers to Iman, not Cally.

C is correct because this detail describes Cally's favorite activity.

D is incorrect because Iman says this, not Cally.

2A

A is incorrect because "asking" is not a synonym of "proposing" as it is used in the sentence.

B is incorrect because "demanding" is not a synonym of "proposing" as it is used in the sentence.

C is incorrect because "guessing" is not a synonym of "proposing" as it is used in the sentence.

D is correct because the paragraph refers to Max offering a suggestion to the group.

2B

A is incorrect because the sentence does not offer any context clues for the meaning of "proposing."

B is incorrect because the sentence does not offer any context clues for the meaning of "proposing."

C is incorrect because the sentence is a detail that explains why Max is proposing something, not the proposal itself.

D is correct because the sentence refers to Max's proposal for the group.

3A

A is incorrect because this statement does not explain how Iman knows the speaker well.

B is incorrect because this statement does not explain how Iman knows the speaker well.

C is incorrect because this statement shows how Iman knows all the group members, not the speaker.

D is correct because this statement shows how Iman knows that the speaker will bring up the topic of sports.

3B

A is incorrect because this sentence refers to Iman, not the speaker.

B is incorrect because this sentence does not refer to how Iman knows the speaker well.

C is correct because this sentence shows that Iman knows what the speaker was going to say.

D is incorrect because this sentence does not refer to how Iman knows the speaker well.

4

A is incorrect because there are no context clues to support "center" as what a zoologist studies.

B is correct because "working with animals" is a context clue that supports that a zoologist studies animals.

C is incorrect because there are no context clues to support "roads" as what a zoologist studies.

D is incorrect because there are no context clues to support "problems" as what a zoologist studies.

5
See answer key for sample response.

6

A is correct because asteroids are "small objects in the sky," which appear star-like when looking at them from Earth.

B is incorrect because the word parts of "asteroid" do not suggest that the word means "like an astronaut."

C is incorrect because the word parts of "asteroid" do not suggest that the word means "planets."

D is incorrect because the word parts of "asteroid" do not suggest that the word means "stars."

7
"Space holds the answers to many questions, and it is vital that we keep trying to find those answers" is correct because this sentence best shows that the author thinks space exploration is necessary.

8

A is incorrect because the author does not organize the passage by describing the history of space exploration.

B is incorrect because the author does not organize the passage by comparing the positives and negatives of space exploration.

C is correct because the author organizes the passage by listing the reasons why it is important to explore space.

D is incorrect because the author does not organize the passage by explaining how we can explore space today.

9A

A is incorrect because the word "unusual" is not an antonym for "invaluable"; they do not have opposite meanings.

B is correct because "unimportant" is the opposite of "invaluable," which means "priceless"; the two words are antonyms.

C is incorrect because "hidden" does not have the opposite meaning of "invaluable."

D is incorrect because "treasured" is similar in meaning to "invaluable," rather than opposite in meaning.

9B

A is incorrect because it does not provide a context clue to the meaning of the world "invaluable."

B is correct because it provides a context clue to the meaning of the world "invaluable."

C is incorrect because it does not provide a context clue to the meaning of the world "invaluable."

D is incorrect because it does not provide a context clue to the meaning of the world "invaluable."

10

"It's in Our Nature" matches with "Examples of ways we explore the world around us" because this heading contains similar information.

"The Creation of Our World" matches with "Examples of places on Earth that have been explored" because this heading contains similar information.

"Inventions" matches with "Examples of things that have been developed during explorations" because this heading contains similar information.

"Unanswered Questions" matches with "Examples of things we don't know about" because this heading contains similar information.

11

"ocean" is the correct answer because the ocean is located on the coast.

13

A is incorrect because it shows no evidence of Carson being a friend of nature.

B is incorrect because it shows no evidence of Carson being a friend of nature.

C is correct because it shows how Carson took action to protect nature, proving her to be a friend of it.

D is incorrect because it shows no evidence of Carson being a friend of nature.

14A

A is incorrect because there is no evidence that Carson would learn chemistry in a biology class.

B is incorrect because there is no evidence that Carson would learn about microscopes in a biology class.

C is incorrect because there is no evidence that Carson would learn about textbooks in a biology class.

D is correct because there is evidence in the passage that Carson would learn plants and animals in a biology class.

14B

A is correct because it describes what Carson learned about in her biology class.

B is incorrect because it does not describe what Carson learned about in her biology class.

C is incorrect because it does not describe what Carson learned about in her biology class.

D is incorrect because it does not describe what Carson learned about in her biology class.

15A

A is incorrect because it does not convince readers to take better care of the environment.

B is correct because it convinces readers to take care of the environment or there will be no more animals to enjoy.

C is incorrect because it does not convince readers to take better care of the environment.

D is incorrect because it does not state a reason for why readers should take better care of the environment.

15B

A is incorrect because it does not show evidence for convincing the reader to take better care of the environment.

B is incorrect because it does not show evidence for convincing the reader to take better care of the environment.

C is incorrect because it does not show evidence for convincing the reader to take better care of the environment.

D is correct because it is a powerful argument for why readers should take better care of the environment.

16

A is incorrect because "write" does not agree with the verb "have."

B is incorrect because "wrote" does not agree with the verb "have."

C is correct because "written" agrees with the verb "have."

D is incorrect because "writed" is not a proper construction of "to write."

17

A is incorrect because it does not fit within the context of the sentence.

B is correct because "can use" fits within the context of the sentence.

C is incorrect because it does not fit within the context of the sentence.

D is incorrect because it does not fit within the context of the sentence.

18

A is incorrect because this is not the proper way to contract "cannot."

B is incorrect because this is not the proper way to contract "cannot."

C is incorrect because this is not the proper way to contract "cannot."

D is correct because "can't" is the proper way to contract "cannot."

19

A is incorrect because this is the past progressive, not the past tense of the verb.

B is incorrect because this is the present, not the past tense of the verb.

C is incorrect because this is the past perfect, not the past tense of the verb.

D is correct because this is the past tense of "to present."

20

A is incorrect because this verb changes the meaning of the sentence.

B is correct because it is in the present tense and agrees with the subject "the cider."

C is incorrect because it does not agree with the subject "the cider."

D is incorrect because this verb is not in the present tense.

Unit 4 Answer Key

Student Name: _____

Question	Correct Answer	Content Focus	Complexity
1A	A	Latin Roots	DOK 2
1B	B	Latin Roots/Text Evidence	DOK 2
2	A, C	Text Structure: Cause and Effect	DOK 2
3	see below	Text Structure: Cause and Effect	DOK 3
4A	D	Context Clues: Synonyms	DOK 2
4B	B	Context Clues: Synonyms/Text Evidence	DOK 2
5	A, C	Text Features: Boldface Words	DOK 2
6	D	Point of View	DOK 2
7	see below	Latin Roots	DOK 2
8	B	Theme	DOK 3
9	see below	Context Clues: Synonyms	DOK 2
10	A	Context Clues: Synonyms	DOK 2
11	D	Context Clues: Synonyms	DOK 2
12	B	Literary Elements: Stanzas	DOK 2
13A	C	Point of View	DOK 2
13B	A	Point of View/Text Evidence	DOK 2
14A	A	Theme	DOK 3
14B	A	Theme/Text Evidence	DOK 3
15	see below	Literary Elements: Repetition	DOK 3
16	D	Pronoun-Verb Agreement	DOK 1
17	A	Possessive Pronouns	DOK 1
18	A	Contractions and Possessives	DOK 1
19	C	Pronouns and Antecedents	DOK 1
20	B	Pronouns and Homophones	DOK 1

Unit 4 Answer Key   Student Name: _____

Comprehension 2, 3, 5, 6, 8, 12. 13A, 13B, 14A, 14B, 15	/18	%
Vocabulary 1A, 1B, 4A, 4B, 7, 9, 10, 11	/12	%
English Language Conventions 16, 17, 18, 19, 20	/5	%
Total Unit 4 Assessment Score	/35	%

3 Students should match the following:

- Bessie read about the Wright brothers and Harriet Quimby.
  Bessie began to think about becoming a pilot.
- No flying school in the United States would take an African American woman.
  Bessie attended flight school in France.
- Bessie dreamed about opening a flight school everyone could attend.
  Bessie began performing in air shows to make money.

7 Students should underline the following word: sound

9 Students should match the following:
- amazing: incredible
- crept: sneaked
- geyser: spout

15 **2-point response:** The author had the two characters running in the race use repeated phrases throughout the poem to stress the differences between the two characters. Tortoise's repeated lines show Tortoise's stick-to-it attitude about running the race, while Hare's repeated lines show how flashy Hare was and his obvious physical advantage over Tortoise.

Unit 4 Answer Key   Student Name: _____

Narrative Performance Task			
Question	Answer	Complexity	Score
1	see below	DOK 3	/1
2	see below	DOK 3	/2
3	see below	DOK 3	/2
Story	see below	DOK 4	/4 [P/O] /4 [D/E] /2 [C]
Total Score			/15

1. Students should circle the following statements:
   - Source #1: "These stories sometimes also taught important lessons as they passed down from generation to generation."
   - Source #2: "One way people, including Native Americans, have used stars for centuries is to help them find their way."

2. **2-point response:** While Source #2 mentions that Native Americans used the stars to create stories and teach lessons, Source #1 actually provides examples of those stories and how they explained the objects in the sky. By providing these, Source #1 helps the reader better understand what lessons were taught and how they reflect the culture they came from.

3. **2-point response:** "Stories Behind the Stars" describes how Native Americans created stories about the sky to help explain its mysteries. They also used these stories about the stars to teach important lessons. "Let the Stars Be Your Guide" includes information about how people and animals relied on the stars and other objects in the sky to navigate.

10-point anchor paper: Long ago, when the stars were first in the sky, none of them moved. They just sat where they were, some arranged into the beginnings of pictures and some scattered randomly. During this time, Fox and Coyote went for a walk and got lost.

"Are we going the right way? I don't recognize the smells here," said Fox.

"I'm sure I'll recognize something soon," answered Coyote.

But the farther they went, the more certain they became that they were lost. Finally, they just sat down and howled at the top of their lungs for help.

Woodpecker heard them. "I will fly high above the trees to look for your home," she said. So she flew and flew. Finally, she found the valley where Fox and Coyote lived. She picked up a stone and placed it in the sky to mark the spot. In the process, she bumped the sky and set all the other stars spinning.

The stone that Woodpecker placed became the North Star, and to this day, it still marks the same spot, while all the other stars spin around it. Woodpecker used it to guide Fox and Coyote home, and other people and animals have used it to find their way ever since.

Unit 4 Rationales

1A

A is correct because the root "pop" means "people."

B is incorrect because the root "pop" does not mean "soda."

C is incorrect because the root "pop" does not mean "love."

D is incorrect because the root "pop" does not mean "a lot."

1B

A is incorrect because it does not support the idea that "pop" means "people."

B is correct because the result of Bessie Coleman becoming popular meant that she became a hero with the people.

C is incorrect because it does not support the idea that "pop" means "people."

D is incorrect because it does not support the idea that "pop" means "people."

2

A is correct because the author likely used subheadings to indicate the main ideas of each section.

B is incorrect because the author did not likely use subheadings to point out the most important details first.

C is correct because the author likely used subheadings to show the order in which events occurred.

D is incorrect because the author did not likely use subheadings to highlight the themes of the entire passage.

E is incorrect because the author did not likely use subheadings to focus on why learning to fly was so important.

3

"Bessie read about the Wright brothers and Harriet Quimby" matches with "Bessie began to think about becoming a pilot" because the first event causes the second.

"No flying school in the United States would take an African American woman" matches with "Bessie attended flight school in France" because the first event causes the second.

"Bessie dreamed about opening a flight school everyone could attend" matches with "Bessie began performing in air shows to make money" because the first event causes the second.

4A

A is incorrect because "airplane" is not a synonym for "aviator."

B is incorrect because "flying" is not a synonym for "aviator."

C is incorrect because "machine" is not a synonym for "aviator."

D is correct because "pilot" is a synonym for "aviator."

4B

A is incorrect because it is not a context clue for the sentence in part A.

B is correct because it is a context clue that relates to the sentence in part A.

C is incorrect because it contains no clues to the meaning of the word "aviator."

D is incorrect because it contains no clues to the meaning of the word "aviator."

5

A is correct because the author explains how Bessie Coleman earned her nickname under the heading "Queen Bess."

B is incorrect because Bessie Coleman never became a queen.

C is correct because the author uses the boldface text to indicate it as a title for the next heading.

D is incorrect because the author has already told how Bessie Coleman learned to fly.

E is incorrect because how Bessie Coleman was killed is not the main point of the paragraph.

6

A is incorrect because an outside observer, not Walter Gilbert, is the narrator of this story.

B is incorrect because an outside observer, not Mrs. Gilbert, is the narrator of this story.

C is incorrect because an outside observer, not Mr. Hamill, is the narrator of this story.

D is correct because an outside observer is the narrator of this story.

7

"Sound" is correct because it gives a clue to the meaning of the word "audible."

8

A is incorrect because the theme of the story is not about Earth's gifts.

B is correct because the message of the story is not to give up because of what others say.

C is incorrect because the theme of the story is not about how hard work leads to success.

D is incorrect because the theme of the story is not about the bond between a mother and son.

9

"Amazing" matches with "incredible" because they have nearly the same meaning.

"Crept" matches with "sneaked" because they have nearly the same meaning.

"Geyser" matches with "spout" because they have nearly the same meaning.

10

A is correct because "saw" is a synonym for "witnessed."

B is incorrect because "believed" is not a synonym for "witnessed."

C is incorrect because "believed" is not a synonym for "witnessed."

D is incorrect because "believed" is not a synonym for "witnessed."

11

A is incorrect because "bright" is not a synonym for "plodding."

B is incorrect because "frisky" is not a synonym for "plodding."

C is incorrect because "charming" is not a synonym for "plodding."

D is correct because "steady" is a synonym for "plodding."

12

A is incorrect because although the dash is used in Hare's stanzas, an entire stanza is repeated.

B is correct because Hare's stanzas are repeated.

C is incorrect because although the length of the lines in some of Hare's stanzas is the same, the entire stanza is repeated.

D is incorrect because although the number of rhyming words in some of Hare's stanzas is the same, the entire stanza is repeated.

13A

A is incorrect because Hare speaks in first-person point of view.

B is incorrect because Mouse speaks in first-person point of view.

C is correct because Reporter speaks in third-person point of view.

D is incorrect because Tortoise speaks in first-person point of view.

13B

A is correct because it is written in third-person point of view.

B is incorrect because it is written in first-person point of view.

C is incorrect because it is written in first-person point of view.

D is incorrect because it is written in first-person point of view.

14A

A is correct because the Tortoise wins the race as a result of never giving up.

B is incorrect because there is no evidence that Hare has learned from his mistakes.

C is incorrect because there is no evidence of a character putting all their eggs in one basket.

D is incorrect because there is no evidence of a character biting off more than they can chew.

14B

A is correct because it shows Tortoise never giving up on trying to win the race.

B is incorrect because this detail shows that Hare gives up on the race.

C is incorrect because this detail shows that Hare gives up on the race.

D is incorrect because it only states how far Tortoise has traveled.

15

See answer key for sample response.

A is incorrect because the verb does not agree with the subject "we."

B is incorrect because the verb does not agree with the subject "we."

C is incorrect because the verb does not agree with the subject "we."

D is correct because the verb agrees with the subject "we."

17

A is correct because the possessive pronoun agrees with its antecedent "Nita."

B is incorrect because the possessive pronoun does not agree with the antecedent "Nita."

C is incorrect because the possessive pronoun does not agree with the antecedent "Nita."

D is incorrect because the possessive pronoun does not agree with the antecedent "Nita."

18

A is correct because this sentence requires a possessive pronoun.

B is incorrect because this sentence requires a possessive pronoun.

C is incorrect because this sentence requires a possessive pronoun.

D is incorrect because this is not the correct form of possessive pronoun for this sentence.

19

A is incorrect because this sentence requires a subject pronoun.

B is incorrect because this sentence requires a subject pronoun.

C is correct because this sentence requires a subject pronoun.

D is incorrect because this sentence requires a subject pronoun.

20

A is incorrect because this sentence requires both a subject and a verb.

B is correct because the contraction "you're" gives the sentence both a subject and a verb.

C is incorrect because this sentence requires both a subject and a verb.

D is incorrect because this sentence requires both a subject and a verb.

Unit 5 Answer Key   Student Name: _____

Question	Correct Answer	Content Focus	Complexity
1A	C	Context Clues: Antonyms	DOK 2
1B	C	Context Clues: Antonyms/Text Evidence	DOK 2
2	A, E	Context Clues: Antonyms	DOK 2
3	A	Homographs	DOK 2
4A	C	Text Structure: Sequence	DOK 2
4B	B	Text Structure: Sequence/Text Evidence	DOK 2
5	see below	Text Structure: Problem and Solution	DOK 2
6A	C, D	Figurative Language: Similes and Metaphors	DOK 3
6B	A	Figurative Language: Similes and Metaphors/Text Evidence	DOK 3
7A	C, D	Context Clues: Antonyms	DOK 2
7B	C	Context Clues: Antonyms/Text Evidence	DOK 2
8	see below	Character, Setting, Plot: Problem and Solution	DOK 3
9A	D	Proverbs and Adages	DOK 2
9B	D	Proverbs and Adages/Text Evidence	DOK 2
10	see below	Character, Setting, Plot: Problem and Solution	DOK 3
11	B	Text Structure: Sequence	DOK 1
12	B	Text Structure: Sequence	DOK 2
13	A	Text Features: Sidebars	DOK 2
14	see below	Text Features: Sidebars	DOK 2
15A	C	Text Structure: Sequence	DOK 2
15B	C	Text Structure: Sequence/Text Evidence	DOK 2
16	D	Proper Adjectives	DOK 1
17	A	Adjectives That Compare	DOK 1
18	B	Combining Sentences	DOK 1
19	A	Demonstrative Adjectives	DOK 1
20	A	Comparing with More and Most	DOK 1

Unit 5 Answer Key   Student Name: _____

Comprehension 4A, 4B, 5, 8, 10, 11, 12, 13, 14, 15A, 15B	/18	%
Vocabulary 1A, 1B, 2, 3, 6A, 6B, 7A, 7B, 9A, 9B	/12	%
English Language Conventions 16, 17, 18, 19, 20	/5	%
Total Unit 5 Assessment Score	/35	%

5 Students should match the following:
- path through the mountains: Wagon trains had more trouble following this path. There were mountain peaks.
- path through the desert: Less water was available on this path. The land was flatter

8 Students should underline the following sentences:
- Maya and I went to the middle of the classroom and began signing to each other.
- It did not take long for students to notice and one by one, they stopped talking to watch us.

10 **2-point response:** The author addresses the problem that sometimes plans go wrong and people need help. In the passage, Katherine's help solves a big problem for both Mr. Park and Maya and makes the first day of school much more pleasant for Maya.

14 Students should match the following:
- conductor: copper, iron, steel
- insulator: plastic, rubber, wood

Unit 5 Answer Key   Student Name: _____

Informational Performance Task			
Question	Answer	Complexity	Score
1	see below	DOK 2	/1
2	see below	DOK 3	/2
3	see below	DOK 3	/2
Informational Article	see below	DOK 3	/4 [P/O] /4 [E/E] /2 [C]
Total Score			/15

1   Students should circle the following:
   - Source #1: These include hand sanitizer, ear buds, a subway card, and popular websites saved on a flash drive.
   - Source #2: Remains can tell us what types of food were eaten, how long people lived, how people spent their days, the sizes of families, and more.

2   **2-point response:** Source #1 mentions how time capsules included all kinds of clues, from financial reports to campaign buttons. The quote from Dr. Yablon points out that the contents of many time capsules are disappointing because they "do not always lead to new knowledge." Source #2 focuses on the types of clues archaeologists use to understand the past but emphasize that clues are found in many places from in the ground to under the water.

3   **2-point response:** Looking into the past is important for a number of reasons. First, as it says in Source #2, it helps people understand where, when, why, and how people lived in the past. Secondly, it shows how information was passed from one generation to the next. In addition, as stated in Source #3, learning about the past and one's descendants helps people learn about and appreciate their cultural heritage.

Unit Assessments   Grade 4 • Unit 5 Answer Key

Unit 5 Answer Key

Student Name: _____

10-point anchor paper: People can learn about the past in many ways. They can learn about their own family history or about the history of the country. They can use different sources to learn different things about the past.

One way people can learn about the past is by looking at things meant for future people to find. Some people created time capsules, which are containers of things collected to help future people understand the past. The passage "A Moment in Time" explains that the things in a time capsule could be financial reports, photographs, political campaign buttons, newspaper articles, or websites saved on a flash drive. Time capsules can be buried underground or in hidden places in buildings until they are found in the distant future. They can even be sent into space. But time capsules are often disappointing because they do not necessarily reveal anything that people didn't already know about the past.

Another way people can learn about the past is by digging up artifacts, like tools, garbage, or the remains of buildings from long ago. This can tell us how people from the past ate, where and how long they lived, the size of their families, what technology they developed and when, and how they treated one another. The passage "Digging into the Past" explains how archaeologists dig for artifacts left behind and study the words written by cultures that had a written language. Archaeologists even study artifacts from underwater, such as shipwrecks. They also study industrial materials from long ago to learn how industry changed over time.

A third way people can learn about the past is by researching their own family history. The passage "Family History" tells how people can interview their own relatives, look at old family record books, check libraries for old directories and newspapers, and look at online databases. They can even pay someone else to research their family history. By learning about their family history, people may learn about their medical history, discover famous relatives, or get in touch with relatives they did not know about before.

Learning about the past is important because it helps people learn about the present. No matter whether people are researching their own family histories, digging for artifacts, or opening time capsules, they are trying to find out more about how the past shaped the present.

Unit 5 Rationales

1A

A is incorrect because "better" is not an antonym of "riskier."

B is incorrect because "easier" is not an antonym of "riskier."

C is correct because "safer" is an antonym of "riskier."

D is incorrect because "wilder" is not an antonym of "riskier."

1B

A is incorrect because this detail offers no context clues as to the meaning of "riskier."

B is incorrect because this detail offers no context clues as to the meaning of "riskier."

C is correct because it offers clues that the second path is different than the first path.

D is incorrect because this detail offers no context clues as to the meaning of "riskier."

2

A is correct because it is an antonym of the word "prohibited" as it is used in the sentence.

B is incorrect because it is a synonym of the word "prohibited."

C is incorrect because it is not an antonym of the word "prohibited" as it is used in the sentence.

D is incorrect because it is not an antonym of the word "prohibited" as it is used in the sentence.

E is correct because it is an antonym of the word "prohibited" as it is used in the sentence.

3

A is correct because "narrow route or road" is similar to "pass" as it is used in the sentence.

B is incorrect because "throw a ball, as in football" is not similar to "pass" as it is used in the sentence.

C is incorrect because "permission to come and go" is not similar to "pass" as it is used in the sentence.

D is incorrect because "move past or around something" is not similar to "pass" as it is used in the sentence.

4A

A is incorrect because this event does not happen first in the passage.

B is incorrect because this event does not happen first in the passage.

C is correct because this event happens first in the passage.

D is incorrect because this event does not happen first in the passage.

4B

A is incorrect because it is not text evidence of Pecos Pueblo becoming a trading center happening first in the passage.

B is correct because it is text evidence of Pecos Pueblo becoming a trading center happening first in the passage.

C is incorrect because it is not text evidence of Pecos Pueblo becoming a trading center happening first in the passage.

D is incorrect because it is not text evidence of Pecos Pueblo becoming a trading center happening first in the passage.

5

"Path through the mountains" matches to "Wagon trains had more trouble following this path" and "There were mountain peaks." "Path through the desert" matches to "Less water was available on this path" and "The land was flatter." These matches are correct because these are the descriptions of the problems found on the different paths as written in the passage.

6A

A is incorrect because there is no indication that people were waiting in the hallways in the sentence.

B is incorrect because there is no indication that there were stairs leading up from the hallways in the sentence.

C is correct because the description of the hallways as "like a downtown train station at rush hour" indicates the hallways were noisy.

D is correct because the description of the hallways as "like a downtown train station at rush hour" indicates the hallways were full of students.

E is incorrect because there is no indication that there were announcements over the loudspeaker in the sentence.

6B

A is correct because this detail supports the idea that there are a lot of students and noises in the hallways.

B is incorrect because this detail does not support the idea that there are a lot of students and noises in the hallways.

C is incorrect because this detail does not support the idea that there are a lot of students and noises in the hallways.

D is incorrect because this detail does not support the idea that there are a lot of students and noises in the hallways.

7A

A is incorrect because "alarmed" is not an antonym of "distracted."

B is incorrect because "confused" is not an antonym of "distracted."

C is correct because "focused" is an antonym of "distracted."

D is correct because "interested" is an antonym of "distracted."

E is incorrect because "worried" is not an antonym of "distracted."

7B

A is incorrect because it provides no context clues for the meaning of the word "distracted."

B is incorrect because it provides no context clues for the meaning of the word "distracted."

C is correct because it is text evidence that Mr. Park is distracted and provides context clues for the meaning of the word.

D is incorrect because it provides no context clues for the meaning of the word "distracted."

8

"Maya and I went to the middle of the classroom and began signing to each other."

"It did not take long for students to notice and one by one, they stopped talking to watch us."

These sentences are correct because they are indications of what happened to the noise level in the classroom.

9A

A is incorrect because the adage does not mean that it will rain that morning.

B is incorrect because the adage does not mean that every bad thing is made of silver.

C is incorrect because the adage does not mean that the clouds were silver in color.

D is correct because the adage means "good things can come from bad situations."

9B

A is incorrect because the detail does not provide clues to the meaning of the adage.

B is incorrect because the detail does not provide clues to the meaning of the adage.

C is incorrect because the detail does not provide clues to the meaning of the adage.

D is correct because the detail shows that a good thing is happening because of the bad situation.

10

See answer key for sample response.

11

A is incorrect because this step does not come right before taping wire to the bottom of the battery.

B is correct because just before taping wire to the bottom of the battery, you have to tape another piece of wire to the top.

C is incorrect because the battery is the power source.

D is incorrect because this is the last step in the project.

12

A is incorrect because the passage does not explain why electricity makes things work.

B is correct because the passage lists the steps to take to create an electrical circuit.

C is incorrect because the passage does not convince the reader to keep their devices charged.

D is incorrect because the passage does not describe devices that use electricity.

13

A is correct because the sidebar informs the reader about the materials that do and do not conduct electricity.

B is incorrect because the sidebar doesn't describe the materials needed for the project.

C is incorrect because the sidebar doesn't tell the reader how to use the materials listed.

D is incorrect because the sidebar doesn't explain how to follow the steps of the project.

14

Copper—Conductor; Iron—Conductor; Plastic—Insulator; Rubber—Insulator; Steel—Conductor; Wood—Insulator are the correct answers as they are organized in the sidebar.

15

A is incorrect because this is not the third step in creating a circuit.

B is incorrect because this is not the third step in creating a circuit.

C is correct because it is the third step in creating a circuit.

D is incorrect because this is not the third step in creating a circuit.

16

A is incorrect because "small" does not need to be capitalized in this sentence, and "American" does.

B is incorrect because "town" does not need to be capitalized in this sentence.

C is incorrect because "small" does not need to be capitalized in this sentence.

D is correct because "American" needs to be capitalized in this sentence.

17

A is correct because "smarter" is the comparative form of "smart."

B is incorrect because "more smart" is not the correct comparative form of "smart."

C is incorrect because "most smarter" is not the correct comparative form of "smart."

D is incorrect because "more smarter" is not the correct comparative form of "smart."

18

A is incorrect because the conjunction does not correctly explain the relationship between the two sentences.

B is correct because the use of the word "because" correctly explains the cause and effect relationship of the two sentences.

C is incorrect because the cause and effect are switched in the sentence.

D incorrect because the sentence does not make sense.

19

A is correct because "this" is the proper demonstrative adjective for "town."

B is incorrect because "that" is not the proper demonstrative adjective for "town."

C is incorrect because "these" is not the proper demonstrative adjective for "town."

D is incorrect because "those" is not the proper demonstrative adjective for "town."

20

A is correct because the speaker enjoys listening to the speaker's grandma talk, so "more than anything else" is in the proper place.

B is incorrect because the placement of "most than anything else" changes the meaning of the sentence and is the improper construction.

C is incorrect because the placement of "more than anything else" changes the meaning of the sentence.

D is incorrect because "most" is the improper form of the comparative in this sentence.

Unit 6 Answer Key

Student Name: _____

Question	Correct Answer	Content Focus	Complexity
1A	C	Main Idea and Key Details	DOK 2
1B	D	Main Idea and Key Details/Text Evidence	DOK 2
2	see below	Connotation and Denotation	DOK 2
3A	A	Connotation and Denotation	DOK 2
3B	B	Connotation and Denotation/Text Evidence	DOK 2
4	D	Latin and Greek Prefixes	DOK 2
5	A, E	Text Features: Sidebars	DOK 2
6	A	Literary Elements: Personification	DOK 2
7	A, D	Literary Elements: Imagery	DOK 3
8A	D	Latin and Greek Prefixes	DOK 2
8B	C	Latin and Greek Prefixes/Text Evidence	DOK 2
9A	C	Theme	DOK 2
9B	C	Theme/Text Evidence	DOK 2
10	see below	Literary Elements: Imagery	DOK 3
11A	A	Theme	DOK 3
11B	C	Theme/Text Evidence	DOK 3
12	B	Figurative Language: Metaphors	DOK 2
13	see below	Theme	DOK 3
14	A	Figurative Language: Metaphors	DOK 2
15	B	Literary Elements: Imagery	DOK 2
16	B	Adverbs	DOK 2
17	B	Negatives	DOK 1
18	D	Sentences Using Prepositions	DOK 2
19	C	Prepositions	DOK 1
20	C	*Good* vs. *Well*	DOK 1

Unit 6 Answer Key   Student Name: _____

Comprehension 1A, 1B, 5, 6, 7, 9A, 9B, 10, 11A, 11B, 13, 15	/18	%
Vocabulary 2, 3A, 3B, 4, 8A, 8B, 12, 14	/12	%
English Language Conventions 16, 17, 18, 19, 20	/5	%
Total Unit 6 Assessment Score	/35	%

2   Students should underline the following word: Curious

10 **2-point response:** The author uses imagery to describe what Hattie sees when she visits her relatives in a city. She is experiencing many new sights and sounds, so the author helps the reader understand how different this place is from her home. The paragraph describes the tall brick house with the red front door and the big, soft armchair.

13 Students should match the following:

- People choose to believe what they want.
  "'Doubtless there are other roads.'"
- Few people seek out the truth.
  "the pathway to truth . . . was thickly grown with weeds."
- The truth can be painful or difficult to bear.
  ". . . each weed was a singular knife."

Unit 6 Answer Key   Student Name: _____

Opinion Performance Task			
Question	Answer	Complexity	Score
1	see below	DOK 3	/1
2	see below	DOK 3	/2
3	see below	DOK 3	/2
Opinion Paper	see below	DOK 4	/4 [P/O] /4 [E/E] /2 [C]
Total Score			/15

1. Students should circle the following:
   - Source #1: Many types of fuel used to produce electricity have become more costly and difficult to find.
   - Source #2: As fossil fuels become harder and more expensive to find, renewable energy sources have become more popular.

2. **2-point response:** Source #2 points out that since fossil fuels are getting more expensive and harder to find, it is essential that people explore renewable energy sources. The main types of renewable energy are explained and shown as ways to help the world's energy reserves.

3. **2-point response:** Source #1, "Energy Efficiency and Conservation," explains that energy is needed to run the world, but it is getting harder and more expensive to find. It is essential that people do whatever they can to use less energy, following tips on how to do so. Source #2, "Renewable Energy Sources," also briefly explains how energy is used in the U.S., but then it focuses on sources that are renewable and how these sources can provide energy that is less costly and will not run out.

10-point anchor paper: Our school should reduce its energy usage by using efficient appliances and renewable energy sources. It should also educate students about the importance of saving energy. This will help us in many ways. The school will save money, help keep the air clean, and avoid wasting resources that people may need in the future. Also, students will learn to save energy for the rest of their lives.

The first thing our school should do is replace all the light bulbs and appliances with new ones that use less energy. This is an easy step that will save money right away. The school should look for Energy Star stickers on the appliances it buys to make sure the appliances are efficient.

Unit 6 Answer Key   Student Name: _____

The next thing our school should do is post rules in every classroom to remind everyone to close the windows and doors when the heat or air conditioning is on, open the curtains for sunlight whenever possible, and turn off the lights when leaving the room. The school could even use tools to help students calculate how much energy they are using. This would help students learn how they can make a difference.

The air conditioner is what uses the most electricity in the school. Our school should use renewable resources for this electricity. Renewable resources the school could use include biomass, hydropower, geothermal, wind, or solar power. Biomass energy comes from plants and animals. Hydropower comes from moving water. Geothermal energy comes from inside the earth, and wind and solar power come from the wind and the sun.

However, hydropower and geothermal energy can only be used where there are hydropower and geothermal power plants nearby. Wind energy can only be used where there is a wind farm, and even there, only when the wind is blowing. Solar power can only be used when the sun is shining. Since we want to power the air conditioner, solar power would work well because the sun is usually shining when we need the air conditioner. The school should start using solar power.

By switching to renewable energy sources and being more efficient about energy usage, our school can save a lot of money and make the world a better place. It can also teach students how to do a better job of saving energy in other parts of their lives. It is very important that our school do this to set a good example for how to use energy wisely.

Unit 6 Rationales

1A

A is incorrect because there are no details to support this as the main idea.

B is incorrect because there are not enough details to support this as the main idea.

C is correct because the title and the details in the passage support that the Lascaux caves are a treasure that had been hidden from the world.

D is incorrect because there are not enough details to support this as the main idea.

1B

A is incorrect because it is not a detail that supports the main idea of the passage.

B is incorrect because it is not a detail that supports the main idea of the passage.

C is incorrect because it is not a detail that supports the main idea of the passage.

D is correct because it is a detail that supports the main idea that the caves are a treasure, a window to the past.

2

"Curious" is the correct answer because it has the same connotation as "interested."

3A

A is correct because "very old" has the same connotation as "ancient."

B is incorrect because "old-fashioned" does not have the same connotation as "ancient."

C is incorrect because "out-of-date" does not have the same connotation as "ancient."

D is incorrect because "worn" does not have the same connotation as "ancient."

3B

A is incorrect because it provides no context clues to the meaning of "ancient."

B is correct because it tells the reader that the paintings are very old.

C is incorrect because it provides no context clues to the meaning of "ancient."

D is incorrect because it provides no context clues to the meaning of "ancient."

4

A is incorrect because "discovery" does not mean "came back."

B is incorrect because "discovery" does not mean "opposite of belief."

C is incorrect because "discovery" does not mean "left a place."

D is correct because "discovery" means "something uncovered."

5

A is correct because the sidebar provides information on the size of the Lascaux caves.

B is incorrect because the sidebar does not provide information on where Jacques Marshal is today.

C is incorrect because the sidebar does not provide information on where Lascaux is located.

D is incorrect because the sidebar does not provide information on how the painters made paint.

E is correct because the sidebar provides information on what is shown in the cave paintings.

F is incorrect because the sidebar does not provide information on the tools used to create shadows.

6

A is correct because the sound of gasping indicates that the train was making noises as it stopped.

B is incorrect because there is no indication in "gasped to a halt" that the train was going very fast.

C is incorrect because there is no indication in "gasped to a halt" that the train whistle was blowing.

D is incorrect because there is no indication in "gasped to a halt" that the train was making passengers sick.

7

A is correct because "like people at a crowded party" is an example of imagery.

B is incorrect because this sentence contains no imagery.

C is incorrect because this sentence contains no imagery.

D is incorrect because this sentence contains no imagery.

E is correct because "white monster squatting in the corner" is an example of imagery.

8A

A is incorrect because the prefix "pre-" does not mean "fully."

B is incorrect because the prefix "pre-" does not mean "after."

C is incorrect because the prefix "pre-" does not mean "again."

D is correct because the prefix "pre-" means "before."

8B

A is incorrect because the detail contains no text evidence of the meaning of the word "preheat."

B is incorrect because the detail contains no text evidence of the meaning of the word "preheat."

C is correct because putting the water on the woodstove is text evidence of preheating the water.

D is incorrect because the detail contains no text evidence of the meaning of the word "preheat."

9A

A is incorrect because there is no indication that this is the lesson Hattie learns in the passage.

B is incorrect because there is no indication that this is the lesson Hattie learns in the passage.

C is correct because Hattie's experience with all the new inventions makes her realize that they make life both easier and harder.

D is incorrect because there is no indication that this is the lesson Hattie learns in the passage.

9B

A is incorrect because the sentence is not evidence of the lesson Hattie learns.

B is incorrect because the sentence is not evidence of the lesson Hattie learns.

C is correct because the sentence is evidence that Hattie learns that not all inventions make life easier.

D is incorrect because the sentence is not evidence of the lesson Hattie learns.

10

See answer key for sample response.

11A

A is correct because the speaker in the poem notes that there are other paths that people follow rather than taking the difficult path to truth.

B is incorrect because the speaker notes at the end of the poem that there are other paths to follow.

C is incorrect because the speaker notes that the pathway to truth has not been taken but not that it should not be taken.

D is incorrect because the speaker states the opposite in the poem, suggesting that many people follow the crowd on the easier path rather than pave their own path to truth.

11B

A is incorrect because it is not a detail that supports the main message of the poem.

B is incorrect because it is not a detail that supports the main message of the poem.

C is correct because it is a detail that supports the main message of the poem.

D is incorrect because it is not a detail that supports the main message of the poem.

12

A is incorrect because the knives do not indicate that the path does not exist.

B is correct because the knives suggest that it is painful to walk along the pathway to truth.

C is incorrect because the knives indicate a painful journey, not one full of lies.

D is incorrect because the knives do not indicate the length of the pathway.

13

"People choose to believe what they want" matches with "Doubtless there are other roads" because the alternative path away from truth represents this.

"Few people seek out the truth" matches with "the pathway to truth... was thickly grown with weeds" because the weeds indicate that the path was not often traveled.

"The truth can be painful or difficult to bear" matches with "... each weed was a singular knife" because the knives represent the pain of the truth.

14

A is correct because the paths and roads represent ways of living.

B is incorrect because the paths and roads do not represent trails the speaker likes walking.

C is incorrect because the paths and roads do not represent ways to weed the lawn.

D is incorrect because the paths and roads do not represent ways to walk to the store.

15

A is incorrect because the metaphor is not a synonym.

B is correct because the metaphor creates an image in the mind.

C is incorrect because the metaphor does not give an inanimate object characteristics of a person.

D is incorrect because the metaphor does not compare anything using "like" or "as."

16

A is incorrect because the plane flying is not because of the weather.

B is correct because adding the phrase with the relative adverb "when" to the beginning of sentence 2 connects it to sentence 1.

C is incorrect because adding the adverb "importantly" to the beginning of sentence 2 does not connect it to sentence 1.

D is incorrect because adding the transition "in other words" to the beginning of sentence 2 does not connect it to sentence 1.

17

A is incorrect because the sentence does not contain a double negative.

B is correct because the sentence contains a double negative.

C is incorrect because the sentence does not contain a double negative.

D is incorrect because the sentence does not contain a double negative.

18

A is incorrect because this sentence does not give the reader a better image of how Orville flew the plane.

B is incorrect because this sentence does not give the reader a better image of how Orville flew the plane.

C is incorrect because this sentence does not give the reader a better image of how Orville flew the plane.

D is correct because by adding the prepositional phrase "in the middle of the bottom wing," the reader can imagine where Orville lay down on the plane.

19

A is incorrect because "holding" is correct in the sentence.

B is incorrect because there should be a comma after "place."

C is correct because the preposition "along" needs to be inserted after "move" to explain how the plane moved.

D is incorrect because the preposition "along" needs to be inserted after "move" to explain how the plane moved.

20

A is incorrect because the sentence would not make sense if "It" replaced "The plane."

B is incorrect because the past tense of "to build" is "built."

C is correct because the word should be the adverb "well," as it describes the verb "worked."

D is incorrect because there should be a period at the end of the sentence.